THE ONLY ETHEREUM INVESTING BOOK YOU'LL EVER NEED

An Absolute Beginner's Guide to Building Wealth with ETH and Crypto + How to Make Money from NFTs, DeFi and Layer 2s

FREEMAN PUBLICATIONS

© **Copyright Freeman Publications 2023 - All rights reserved.**

The content contained within this book may not be reproduced, duplicated or transmitted without direct written permission from the author or the publisher.

Under no circumstances will any blame or legal responsibility be held against the publisher, or author, for any damages, reparation, or monetary loss due to the information contained within this book, either directly or indirectly.

Legal Notice:

This book is copyright protected. It is only for personal use. You cannot amend, distribute, sell, use, quote or paraphrase any part, or the content within this book, without the consent of the author or publisher.

Disclaimer Notice:

The following work is presented for informational purposes only. None of the information herein constitutes an offer to sell or buy any security or investment vehicle, nor does it constitute an investment recommendation of a legal, tax, accounting or investment recommendation by Freeman Publications, its employees or paid contributors. The information is presented without regard for individual investment preferences or risk parameters and is general, non-tailored, non-specific information.

Freeman Publications, including all employees and paid contributors, agree not to trade in any security they write about for a minimum of three days (72 hours) following publication of a new article, book, report or email. Except for existing orders that were in place before submission (any such orders will also always be disclosed inside the document). This includes equity, options, debt, or other instruments directly related to that security, stock, or company. The author may have indirect positions in some companies mentioned due to holdings in mutual funds, ETFs, Closed End Funds or other similar vehicles, and there is no guarantee that the author is aware of the individual portfolios of any of those funds at any given time. Such indirect holdings will generally not be disclosed.

Warning: There is no magic formula to getting rich, in the financial markets or otherwise. Investing often involves high risks and you can lose a lot of money. Success in investment vehicles with the best prospects for price appreciation can only be achieved through proper and rigorous research and analysis. Please do not invest with money you cannot afford to lose. The opinions in this content are just that, opinions of the authors. We are a publishing company and the opinions, comments, stories, reports, advertisements and articles we publish are for informational and educational purposes only; nothing herein should be considered personalized investment advice. Before you make any investment, check with your investment professional (advisor). We urge our readers to review the financial statements and prospectus of any company they are interested in. We are not responsible for any damages or losses arising from the use of any information herein. Past performance is not a guarantee of future results.

This work is based on SEC filings, current events, interviews, corporate press releases, and what we've learned as financial journalists. It may contain errors and you shouldn't make any investment decision based solely on what you read here. It is your money and your responsibility.

Freeman Publications Ltd. are 100% independent in that we are not affiliated with any security, investment vehicle, bank or brokerage house.

All registered trademarks are the property of their respective owners.

TABLE OF CONTENTS

HOW TO GET THE MOST OUT OF THIS BOOK

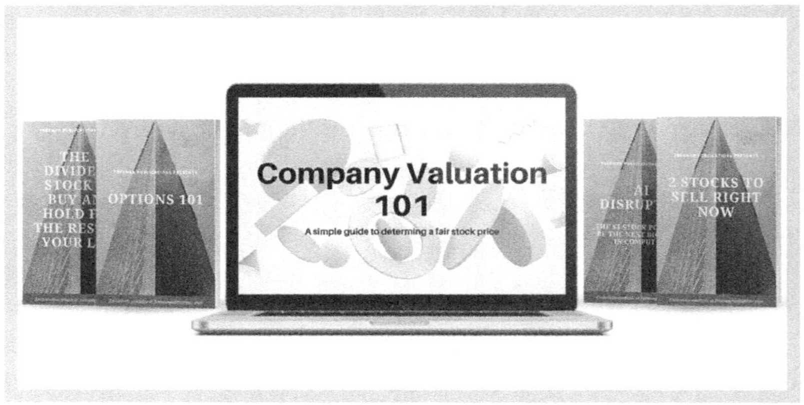

To help you along your investing journey, we've created a free bonus companion course that includes spreadsheets, bonus video content, and additional resources that will help you get the best possible results. We highly recommend you sign up now to get the most out of this book. You can do that by going to the link below or scanning the QR code with your cell phone

https://freemanpublications.com/bonus

Or text the word BONUS to 844-968-4152 (US only)

Free bonus #1: Company Valuation 101 video course ($97 value)

In this 8 part video course, you'll discover our process for accurately valuing a company. This will help you determine if a stock is overvalued, correctly valued, or a bargain. Giving you an indicator of whether to buy or not.

Free bonus #2: Guru Portfolios Analyzed ($37 value)

In these videos, we analyze the stock portfolios of Billionaire investors like Warren Buffett. As well as top entrepreneurs like Bill Gates.

Free bonus #3: Crypto 101 ($47 value)

When you have a paradigm-shifting technology like cryptocurrency and blockchain ... there are multiple ways to profit from it.

But before you rush out and buy every altcoin under the sun... there is a smarter way of doing this.

The ways used by hedge funds and Billionaire investors to make massive profits from the price of Bitcoin and other cryptocurrencies.

And you don't need anything more than a regular brokerage account to do so.

We covered exactly how to do this in a private call for our premium members recently and you'll get access to this video for free.

Free bonus #4: 2 Stocks to Sell Right Now ($17 value)

These 2 stocks are in danger of plummeting in the next 12 months. They're both popular with retail investors, and one is even in the top 5 most held stocks on Robinhood. Believe us; you don't want to be holding these going into 2021 and beyond.

Free bonus #5: AI Disruptor - The $4 Stock Poised to be the Next Big Thing in Computing ($17 value)

This under the radar company, which less than 1% of investors have heard of, is at the forefront of a breakthrough technology that will change our lives as we know them. Soon this technology will be in every smartphone, tablet, and laptop on the planet.

Free bonus #6: Options 101 ($17 Value)

Options don't have to be risky. In fact, they were invented to *reduce* risk. It's no wonder that smart investors like Warren Buffett regularly use options to supplement their long-term portfolio. In this quick start guide, we show you how options work and why they are tools to be utilized rather than feared.

Free bonus #7: The 1 Dividend Stock to Buy and Hold for the Rest of Your Life ($17 Value)

Dividends are the lifeblood of any income investor, and this stock is a cornerstone of any dividend strategy. A true dividend aristocrat with consistent payouts for over 50 years which you'll want to add to your portfolio for sure.

Free bonus #8: All the images inside this book in color ($17 Value)

As much as we'd like to print these books in full color, the printing costs prohibit us from doing so. So on our website, you can get all the images from the book in full color.

Free bonus #9: Our #1 High Yield Stock for 2023 ($17 Value)

A company with a virtual monopoly in its industry. The stock pays a 10% yield while offering capital appreciation. Best of all? It's only $9/share.

All of these bonuses are 100% free, with no strings attached. You don't need to enter any details except your email address.

To get your bonuses go to

https://freemanpublications.com/bonus

Or text the word BONUS to 844-968-4152 (US only)

INTRODUCTION:
CRYPTO IS DEAD, LONG LIVE CRYPTO!

They say a week in crypto feels like a month in the traditional financial markets... and a month in crypto feels like a year. Well, I guess that means a year feels like a decade, and what a year we've had!

These past 12 months have been an absolute minefield of failed projects, scams and regulatory hurdles. Crypto was called "dead" about 450 times by various media outlets, many of whom said the exact opposite during the previous bull market.

We've also had to contend with crypto being usurped by AI as Silicon Valley's favorite plaything. Yet despite all of this (and the crypto market moving faster than Sam Bankman Fried's hands during an interview), here we are. As I write this Ethereum is up around 100% from the previous bear market lows we saw in June 2022, roughly in line with the crypto market as a whole.

If you've been in crypto a while, this likely isn't your first bear market. ETH lost roughly 90% of its value in 2018 alone before soaring 48x from December 2018 to November 2021.

Built by a college dropout with the goal of powering the decentralized internet, Ethereum has now fully cemented itself as the number 2 cryptocurrency after Bitcoin. ETH even outperformed bitcoin's performance in the previous 2 cycles and currently makes up 20% of the overall crypto market.

While the 2020/2021 bull market was dominated by narratives of "Ethereum killers" and blockchains like Solana, Avalanche and Cardano receiving a lot of attention and positive price appreciation.. Ethereum has once again proved to be the strongest of the layer 1 blockchains. Both in terms of overall network activity and token price. The rise of new innovations like NFTs, DeFi and Layer 2s has only helped propel Ethereum and DApps to new heights.

Part technological innovation, and part alterative asset class – it's clear that Ethereum is here to stay on both levels. Having owned Ethereum in my personal portfolio for the past 6 years, I've benefitted handsomely from this asymmetric bet. Freeman Publications subscribers have also done well after we doubled down on our recommendation in June 2022. The latest network upgrades like The Merge and the following Shapella upgrade go further to cement my long-term bullishness on Ethereum.

The goal of this book, like all of our books, is simple. First, help you understand Ethereum on a technological level. Whether it's stock or crypto, you should never invest in anything you don't understand. Secondly, I want to contextualize how Ethereum sits in the wider and blockchain ecosystem today. Then I want to go deeper into the newer innovations that sit on top of the Ethereum blockchain like NFTs, DeFi and Layer 2s – because each of these offers it's own unique profit making potential.

To go further, I should also clarify what this book is not. This is not a quasi-political diatribe under the "ETH Maximalist" party line. I am bullish on both Bitcoin and Ethereum long-term (albeit for different reasons), and have written about my thoughts on the overall crypto ecosystem in previous bestselling books The Only Bitcoin Book You'll Ever Need and The Only Cryptocurrency Investing Book You'll Ever Need. Nor will we examine Ethereum from a developer's standpoint – there are far smarter people than I who can speak on that topic.

Freeman Publications is dedicated to serving the individual investor, and our mission is to ensure regular investors get better returns in the stock market. Hence why this book, and all our books have that as our North Star goal. Since 2020 we've published 13 books, including multiple bestsellers and helped over 125,000 investors - not bad for a self-funded operation with zero help from traditional publishers. We hope this book will do the same for you.

So get comfy, grab a beverage of your choice, and let's dive into the exciting world of Ethereum.

Oliver El-Gorr

Founder & CEO, Freeman Publications

London, England

June 2023

Chapter 01

ETHEREUM - THERE IS MORE TO CRYPTO THAN JUST BITCOIN

Instead of putting the taxi driver out of a job, blockchain puts Uber out of a job and lets the taxi drivers work with the customer directly
- *Vitalik Buterin, Founder of Ethereum.*

In October 2008, when most of the world's economies were busy dealing with the largest financial crisis in decades, something mysterious happened. Out of nowhere, an anonymous person named Satoshi Nakamoto sent a working paper to a cryptography mailing list - setting the stage for more dramatic events and potentially altering the future of money. Titled *Bitcoin: A Peer-to-Peer Electronic Cash System,* the paper introduced distributed blockchain (a decentralized public ledger) and a peer-to-peer payment system that doesn't need a trusted third party. At a time when financial instability shook the confidence of people in the traditional financial system, the promise of a digital currency that would bypass the authority of central banks sounded like a dream come true.

This is the story of Bitcoin - the first-ever cryptocurrency and the crypto poster boy that set the most significant chain reaction of financial innovation in many centuries. To date, we don't have any idea who Satoshi really is (or was?). What we definitely know is that by the time of writing this book, there are nearly 9,000 active cryptocurrencies in the world with a combined market value of more than $1.25 trillion.

But, not everything that shines is gold.

In 2011, Vitalik Buterin, a 17-year old Russian-Canadian programmer, was intrigued by the promises of Bitcoin and co-founded the Bitcoin Magazine the very next year. However, Buterin quickly realized the inherent limitations of Bitcoin, which was purposely designed to suit certain specific cases (like making payments). The system proposed by Satoshi has limited programmability. Therefore, Bitcoin can primarily serve as a medium of exchange (like paying for a pizza) and a store of value (like saving your extra income for the future). But what if we wanted to use this technology to build smartphone-like applications? The Bitcoin network is not equipped to do it. In the words of Buterin, *I thought [those in the Bitcoin community] weren't approaching the problem in the right way. I thought they were going after in•ivi•ual applications; they were trying to kin• of explicitly support each [use case] in a sort of Swiss Army knife protocol.*

Buterin wanted to take the idea of Bitcoin to a whole new level. He started developing a blockchain with its inbuilt programming language to support many more applications - like executing smart contracts (digital contracts that don't need trusted third parties) or building a social network with greater privacy. Paraphrasing the words of Buterin, while Bitcoin offered a specific utility, he wanted to build a 'smartphone' that would run any application we want. The result was Ethereum - a general-purpose and programmable blockchain platform that can potentially become the backbone of Web3 (a decentralized Internet powered by blockchain).

Even though the creation of Ethereum was much less dramatic than that of Bitcoin, the former arguably offers a more exciting future potential than the latter.

Let's explore how.

What is Ethereum?

Bitcoin offers a payment network that can be used to transfer economic values, but Ethereum does much more as it's programmable. Developers can create and deploy decentralized applications using this platform. With Ethereum, the possibilities are endless. Officially launched in 2015, Ethereum is creating the Internet of the future that would not require any single authority.

Let's break all this down into simpler words.

Ethereum.org, the body primarily looking after Ethereum's development, defines Ethereum as *a technology for building apps and organizations, holding assets, transacting, and communicating without being controlled by a central authority.* In technical terms, Ethereum is a general-purpose blockchain (whereas Bitcoin is a specific-purpose one) that can be programmed to develop different applications and services. Think of Ethereum as a technology platform or marketplace offering financial services, immersive games, social networks, or any other application in a secure and decentralized way. This means greater privacy, lower transaction costs, and added security. Moreover, we don't need a different blockchain for every application we want - rather, we can just build whatever application we want on the Ethereum platform itself.

The Ethereum platform has its own cryptocurrency called Ether (ETH). It's like Bitcoin, in that it can be used to transfer economic values on the Ethereum network or used as an asset for investing. When we talk about buying or selling Ethereum, we mean trading Ether (ETH) through a cryptocurrency exchange like Coinbase. People often use these terms interchangeably - which is not correct. Ethereum is more like the US economy while ETH is like the US dollar.

How does Ethereum work?

Ethereum, similar to Bitcoin, is based on blockchain technology. For the uninitiated, a blockchain is a distributed database that records all peer-to-peer transactions in a network of blocks. Distributed means the database is not located at one particular physical location - rather it's shared across a network of computers (called nodes) that maintain and update the database. Each block on a blockchain contains a certain amount of transaction information (along with their time stamps) that can't be deleted or altered. More importantly, a blockchain doesn't require a trusted third party (like government agencies or a central bank) for transactions to take place in a smooth and secure way.

The entire Ethereum platform is based on certain core components:

1. Smart contracts

Smart contracts constitute the heart of the Ethereum platform and they make Ethereum truly unique. Smart contracts are like normal business contracts except they are rule-based and they don't need a governing third party for arbitration. These contracts are programmable agreements on the Ethereum platform, which are executed automatically when the pre-conditions are fulfilled.

The Ethereum smart contracts govern all transactions on the Ethereum network in a trustless way. This means you don't need to trust any authority as contracts are fulfilled as long as conditions are met. The majority of Ethereum's use cases are based on smart contracts. It's because of these smart contracts that Ethereum is the preferred choice for decentralized applications or dApps (more on this in the next chapters).

2. The Ethereum blockchain

The Ethereum blockchain stores transaction information in chronologically ordered blocks on the Ethereum platform in a permanent and unalterable way. Blockchain is a public ledger of transaction data in which transactions are verified and recorded by nodes i.e., network participants. There is no single authority for verifying and storing data on the network so there is no single point of failure. Since its inception, Ethereum has never suffered a network downtime - not a small technological achievement. In comparison, Solana (SOL), which positions itself as the 'Ethereum-killer', suffered at least 6 major outages in 2022 and another one in February 2023.

3. Consensus protocol

In a blockchain, transaction data are verified and stored by the network participants. Since a participant can be anyone with a computer located across diverse geographies, there needs to be a coordination mechanism to agree on data values. This coordination mechanism that leads to agreements in a decentralized environment is called consensus protocol. Think of the consensus protocol as a voting system to arrive at a final decision.

From the beginning, Ethereum, similar to Bitcoin, used the Proof-of-Work (PoW) consensus mechanism. The PoW mechanism is based on mining - solving complex mathematical problems before a participant is able to validate transactions on a block. However, one significant problem with PoW is that it requires humongous computing power to solve these mathematical puzzles. Therefore, blockchains running on PoW are energy intensive, which greatly inhibits their scalability (the ability of the platform to manage an exponentially increasing number of transactions). According to estimates by the University of Cambridge, Bitcoin's annualized energy consumption is 124 terawatt-hours (TWh) a year, which is equal to the annual electricity consumption of Argentina!

Given the limitations of PoW, in September 2022 Ethereum shifted to a relatively new consensus mechanism called Proof of Stake (PoS). In this consensus mechanism, the ability of a node to validate blocks depends on cryptocurrency holding and not computing power. The PoS has higher throughput (number of transactions per unit of time) and scalability along with being extremely energy efficient. According to the Ethereum Foundation's estimates, the shift to PoS has lowered annualized energy consumption of Ethereum by a whopping 99.98%.

4. Ethereum Virtual Machine (EVM)

The EVM is the computing architecture that powers the Ethereum blockchain and smart contracts. While nodes on the Ethereum blockchain validate and keep copies of transaction data, the EVM processes and updates the distributed ledger. The EVM makes the Ethereum network programmable so a programmer can develop any application on it.

5. ETH cryptocurrency

ETH or Ether is the native coin of the Ethereum ecosystem. Like you need fiat currency to make a purchase in the traditional economy, ETH is the currency for any activity on the Ethereum network. It works as an incentive for the participants to validate nodes. You need a certain amount of this currency to participate in the Ethereum network. It can also be used as an asset or a store of economic value like Bitcoin. With a market cap of $228.5 billion (as of May 2023), ETH is the second most valuable cryptocurrency after Bitcoin.

Applications and growth of Ethereum

Ethereum is like a blockchain marketplace that has a growing number of potential applications. Let's first look at these staggering statistics indicating the rapid growth of Ethereum in less than 8 years:

- **The number of daily transactions**: More than 1 million, which is 4 times that of Bitcoin.
- **The number of smart contracts**: 50 million+.
- **The number of projects built on Ethereum**: Around 3,000.
- **The number of user accounts holding ETH**: More than 71 million - higher than the population of France or the UK.
- **Unique addresses on the Ethereum network:** 200 million+, which is greater than the combined population of the UK, France, and Italy.

Ethereum can facilitate peer-to-peer financial transactions without any intermediary. This means you can send or receive funds without the need for a bank or other financial institution. Ethereum's smart contracts enable us to enter into agreements with another party while not having to worry about maintaining escrow or arbitration. The programmed contracts are executed or canceled based on the status of the underlying conditions. Smart contracts can drastically reduce the transaction costs of doing business.

Ethereum is poised to be the backbone of the decentralized Web3 which addresses the privacy issues paralyzing Web 2.0, the Internet we use today. Moreover, Ethereum can be the building block of Decentralized Autonomous Organizations (DAOs) and Decentralised Finance (DeFi) while hosting millions of dApps (gaming, social networking, entertainment, and much more) and supporting new asset classes like Non-Fungible Tokens (NFTs). While these terms may sound quite esoteric at this point, we will explore these applications of Ethereum in greater detail in the next chapters. For now, an important point to take home is that the wider the adoption rate and applicability of the Ethereum ecosystem, the greater would be the investment worthiness of ETH. According to a report by Zion Market Research, the global DeFi market is projected to grow to $232.20 billion by 2030 from a paltry $11.96 billion in 2021. Since Ethereum is the uncontested market leader in DeFi, we can make a fairly educated guess on the huge market potential of Ethereum in the coming years.

Chapter 02

ETHEREUM'S HISTORY IN 10 MINUTES

You never change things by fighting the existing reality.
To change something, build a new model
that makes the existing model obsolete.
- ***Buckminster Fuller**, American architect, inventor, and futurist.*

Like most teenagers, Vitalik Buterin was a great fan of video games. During 2007-10, he was happily playing World of Warcraft until Blizzard abruptly nerfed his character - removing the damage component from the Siphon Life spell.

Great ideas can come from the most unlikely of sources. Legend says that Archimedes discovered the principles of buoyancy while relaxing in his bathtub. Going by another account, the great Isaac Newton came up with his theories on gravity while reflecting on a fallen apple. Taking it with "a pinch of salt", the origin of Ethereum can be traced back to Buterin's disappointment with changes in his favorite online game. Reflecting on this experience, after a couple of years, Buterin wrote - *I cried myself to sleep, and on that day I realized what horrors centralized services can bring. I soon decided to quit.*

Meanwhile, a lot was happening in the Bitcoin space. Satoshi appeared, led the initial developments of Bitcoin, and then mysteriously disappeared in 2010 after putting Gavin Andresen in front to run the show. In 2011, searching for a new purpose in life, I discovered Bitcoin, mused Buterin in a philosophical tone. However, it was not a story of love at first sight. Initially, Buterin was skeptical about the idea of a digital currency having an intrinsic value without being backed by any real asset. Slowly, the idea started sinking in, hooking him fully to the world of cryptos. The next two years were eventful - he wrote weekly Bitcoin blog posts for $1.5 per hour, cofounded the Bitcoin Magazine, and entered University before dropping out in 2013 to devote himself to crypto projects fulltime.

And so the Ethereum story begins…

November 2013 - the Ethereum white paper

Full of new ideas and insights, Buterin, still in his teenage years, was exploring the possibilities of building on Satoshi's ideas and developing a general-purpose blockchain. He consolidated his ideas in a whitepaper released in November 2013. The name Ethereum came from the word Ether - the hypothetical element pervading all spaces in the universe. Ethereum was designed to apply the concept of blockchain to develop a programmable and all-pervading base that would help applications run on the top of it.

Unlike Bitcoin, Buterin's blockchain was not merely a payment system. The Ethereum white paper mentions - *what Ethereum intends to provide is a blockchain with a built-in fully-fledged Turing-complete programming language that can be used to create "contracts" ... allowing users to create any of the systems described above, as well as many others that we have not yet imagined, simply by writing up the logic in a few lines of code.* In simple words, Turing-complete means a system is programable to solve a wide range of problems. Ethereum was envisioned to do everything a component developer can think of.

Once the white paper was out, the next step was to take this idea to more developers and investors.

January 2014 - Buterin announces Ethereum to the world

The following one and a half years were literally globe-trotting for Buterin - networking, attending conferences around the world, and expounding on his ideas on Ethereum. In January 2014, Buterin announced the Ethereum project at the North American Bitcoin Conference in Miami. Even though he was the prominent face of the project, Ethereum considers an unusually long list of developers as its founders. The list includes the initial 5 (Vitalik Buterin, Anthony Di Iorio, Charles Hoskinson, Mihai Alisie, and Amir Chetrit), as well as Joseph Lubin, Gavin Wood, & Jeffrey Wilcke who joined later in 2014. Most of them attended the Miami conference.

Following Buterin's initial announcement, the Ethereum project was successful in creating enough media hype. It was touted as "Bitcoin for everything." By the end of January, tech-focused magazine WIRED ran a detailed news story with the headline - *Out in the Open: Teenage Hacker Transforms Web Into One Giant Bitcoin Network.* The article ended with an optimistic view on the project - *Ethereum an• other next-gen crypto-platforms paint a very attractive picture of our online future, one where users are in control, not governments or big companies. Buil•ing this future is an enormous task, but Vitalik Buterin woul•n't have it any other way.*

In Buterin, the crypto world got a new hero.

By mid 2014, the Ethereum team met again in Zug, Switzerland when they decided to move forward as a non-profit organization. Subsequently, the Ethereum Foundation was established as a Swiss non-profit foundation. Gavin Wood, who later co-founded Polkadot (DOT), led the initial technical developments at Ethereum. He served as the Chief Technology Officer (CTO) and developed the Ethereum Yellow Paper. The paper defined the Ethereum Virtual Machine (EVM) and the Ethereum protocol (set of rules governing the Ethereum platform).

July 2014 - Initial Coin Offering (ICO)

Ether (ETH) went for an initial crowdfunding in July 2014 to raise funds for further development - and to reward the founders, early developers, and investors. Buyers could exchange their bitcoins for ETH, which is required for all transactions on the Ethereum network. The initial price was fixed at 1 bitcoin for 2,000 Ether. The ICO received tremendous response from tech enthusiasts around the globe - raising approx. $2.2 million in just 12 hours. By the end of the sale, which went on for 42 days, 50 million ETH were sold raising more than $17.3 million. This was a great relief for the team which almost depleted all their funds working on the projects for the last several months. In a controversial step, 9.9% of the ETH was set aside for the founding members whereas another 9.9% was given to the Ethereum Foundation.

Remember that these ETH were not usable until the genesis block (the first block in a blockchain) was created later in 2015. In fact, there was no ETH before the creation of the genesis block. This type of creation and sale of cryptos to the public before a blockchain goes live is called pre-mining.

July 2015 - Ethereum goes live

Ethereum's public launch was initially planned for the winter of 2014/15. For the whole of 2014 and half of 2015, developers at Ethereum came up with several test network prototypes with interesting names like Olympic and Frontier. The Ethereum network was officially launched on July 30, 2015 when the genesis block was created. 8893 transactions were recorded in the Genesis block - most of which involved transferring ETH to various addresses.

Ethereum's official launch was a much-awaited crypto event of the year. The following day, a headline from TechCrunch read - *Vapor No More: Ethereum Has Launched*. The columnist John Evan signed off with the following remarks - *congratulations are in order to its founder (and Thiel*

Fellow) Vitalik Buterin, an• the rest of its team. They have built an• shippe• something genuinely new, extraor•inarily ambitious, an• intellectually fascinating. That's much more than most startups can say.

But ambitions become realities only through the test of time.

2016 - The year of crises

Most novel technologies tend to have a weak point - the Achilles heel that is vulnerable to attacks. In June 2016, it became obvious that Ethereum was not an exception. Friday, June 17, 2016, a hacker stole ETH worth $60 million exploiting a coding loophole in a smart contract. The event, commonly known as the DAO Attack, sent a shockwave across the Ethereum community. How did this happen? Let's simplify.

One of the defining features of Ethereum is a smart contract that enables parties to transact in a trustless environment. The smart contracts on Ethereum enable new-age organizations called Decentralized Autonomous Organizations (DAOs). These organizations don't need governing authorities and their transactions are based on programmed rules.

In May 2016, some developers on the Ethereum platform envisioned 'The DAO' - a special-purpose entity designed to act as a venture capital firm. So anyone with a business idea could pitch to the community and receive funds from the DAO. Lauded as a revolutionary project, the DAO was able to raise $150 million from more than 11,000 investors in just 3 weeks - making it one of the largest crowdfunding campaigns ever. However, even before the token sale was complete, an attacker found a loophole in DAO's code. It was possible to drain DAO's funds through this loophole.

In simpler words, the bug made it possible to withdraw Ether multiple times before the balance was updated on the smart contract. Within the first few hours, the attacker was able to siphon out 3.6 million ETH (equivalent to more than $60 million). Faced with a huge crisis,

Ethereum's community took control of the situation with a war-time urgency. The hacker was unable to pull off the last leg of its heist as the Ethereum community put the funds on hold for a period of 28 days.

The Ethereum community contemplated multiple solutions for the DAO attack. After days of deliberation, it was decided that a hard fork would be conducted on the Ethereum network. A hard fork takes place when a blockchain gets divided into two branches because of a radical shift in the protocol. Through this fork, Ethereum's history was rolled back to before the attack, and DAO's Ether was reallocated to a different branch of the blockchain. In layman's terms, the new branch reflected that there was never any heist!

Ethereum's history was shifted to a new track.

However, this step did not go down well with the purists who insisted on the immutability principle (all transactions are recorded permanently) of blockchain. This section of the Ethereum community stuck to the old chain. As a result, two branches of the Ethereum network exist today - the original blockchain named Ethereum Classic (ETC), and the new Ethereum blockchain that we know as today's Ethereum.

The DAO attack put Ethereum in an existential crisis. Many quickly started writing off Ethereum or even the entire blockchain technology. The prestigious New York Times went on to write - *A Hacking of More Than $50 Million Dashes Hopes in the World of Virtual Currency.*

Even though the network faced another attack in 2016, it was not the end of Ethereum.

2017 - Present: cementing itself as the no. 2

After a crisis-ridden 2016, the year 2017 was a particularly good one for Ethereum. A significant development in the year was the creation of the Enterprise Ethereum Alliance. It's a global community of leaders, adopters, innovators, developers, and businesses promoting the Ethereum platform. Set up in 2017 with 30 founding members, the alliance has grown to include more than 100 members at present with companies like Microsoft, Accenture, Ernst & Young, and FedEx.

The Alliance took Ethereum's popularity to a new height. ETH, which was trading at $100 in May 2017, reached the value of $774.69 by the end of 2017 to become the second most-valued cryptocurrency. Over the years, ETH has cemented this position. With the last trading price of $1,898 (as of May 5, 2023), ETH's current market cap is $228.5 billion - compared to market leader Bitcoin's $566.3 billion valuation.

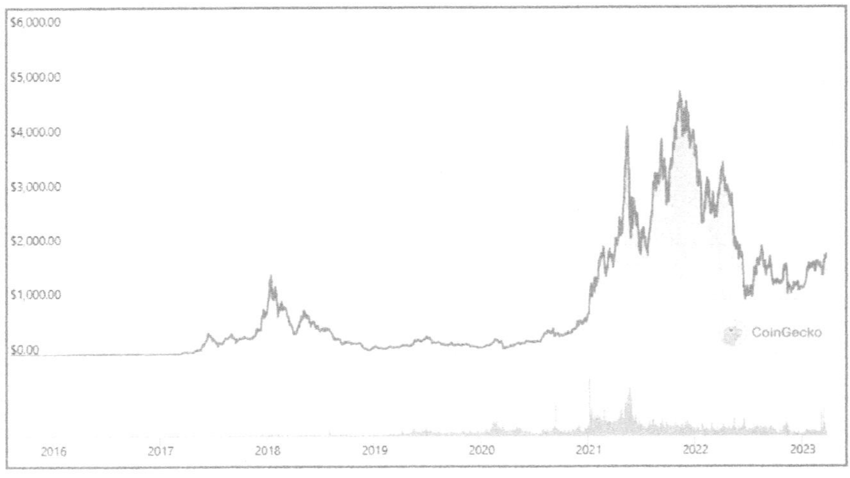

Figure 1: *ETH's price history (Source: CoinGecko)*

Since 2017, the Ethereum network has undergone several upgrades to make the network more scalable, secure, and efficient while lowering transaction costs. The latest and the largest of these upgrades was the 'Merge' which took place in September 2022. This upgrade resulted in Ethereum's shift from Proof-of-Work (PoW) to Proof-of-Stake (PoS). The former relies on energy-intensive computing while the latter is based on staking ETH to validate blocks. Post Merge, Ethereum's annual energy consumption is 0.0026 terawatt-hours (TWh) compared to Netflix's 94 TWh. Quite evidently, this upgrade resolves the scalability issue of Ethereum to some extent. Although a lot more is planned for future upgrades.

We will discuss the most important Ethereum upgrades in detail in the next chapters. But before that, let's explore how Ethereum's ecosystem differs from that of Bitcoin.

Chapter 03

COMPARING ETHEREUM WITH BITCOIN - SIMILARITIES AND DIFFERENCES

Bitcoin is first and foremost a currency; this is one particular application of a blockchain. However, it is far from the only application ... e-mail is one particular use of the Internet, and for sure helped popularize it, but there are many others.
*- **Gavin Wood,** Cofounder of Ethereum and Polkadot.*

November 2015 - Bitcoin, with about 90% of the total crypto market capitalization, is synonymous with crypto while Ethereum was just another promising new kid on the block. In the previous month, the European Court of Justice recognized Bitcoin as a legitimate payment mechanism and exempted it from value-added taxes while exchanging with traditional currencies. The landmark judgment gave a huge boost to Bitcoin-based transactions. Global corporate behemoths like Goldman Sachs were integrating the Bitcoin network to augment their services. Then, Microsoft did something markedly different from others. The tech giant announced its partnership with Ethereum-based application provider ConsenSys to offer Ethereum Blockchain as a Service (EBaaS) on Microsoft Azure, its cloud computing platform.

So why did Microsoft choose Ethereum and not the well-established Bitcoin? Microsoft's reply was - *While a platform like Bitcoin has many great uses specifically as a cryptocurrency, Ethereum provi•es the flexibility an• extensibility many of our customers were looking for. But that is just scratching the surface of what can be •one when you mix the cryptographic security an• reliability of the blockchain with a Turing-complete programming language inclu•e• in Ethereum, we can't really imagine what our customers an• partners will buil•.*

Microsoft's reply pretty much sums up this chapter.

While Bitcoin provides a particular app, Ethereum has the entire app store to offer. Bitcoin is mainly designed as a secure peer-to-peer payment system while Ethereum is more like a build-as-you-like blockchain platform. Both have a few similarities and a whole lot of differences. So, which one is better? Are they mutually exclusive or can they coexist? Which one has a greater investment potential?

Let's dig deeper.

The few similarities

In 1991, research scientists Stuart Haber and Scott Stornetta at Bellcore Labs had a puzzle to solve - authenticating digital documents to preserve the originals. All the solutions they could come up with needed a trusted third party to certify authenticity. And how does one ensure that the trusted party is actually trustworthy? By adding another independent body (the 4th party) and so on? Apparently, the solution lay somewhere else.

After weeks of brainstorming, they found a way to timestamp documents and preserve their authenticity through novel technology. This was the birth of blockchain. Decades later, Stornetta, in an interview with CoinGeek, revealed - *We expecte• all the worl•'s financial recor•s woul• be •one with this system. But in a••ition, all the worl•'s photographs, all the worl•'s movies. So we weren't short on ambition.* Clearly, blockchain could be used to solve a large number of real-world problems. However, quite surprisingly, there were not many takers of this new technology. It went on years of hibernation until it reemerged with a bang.

17 years later, Satoshi Nakamoto built on this early notion of blockchain to make it truly decentralized and use it in a very specific case - peer-to-peer payment. Vitalik Buterin, on the other hand, took Satoshi's blockchain to align it more with the original intention of Haber and Stornetta - applying it to a broad range of problems. To cut the long story short, both Bitcoin and Ethereum are the results of the same streams of technology - blockchain, peer-to-peer transactions, cryptography, and decentralization.

So both these platforms have the same or similar building blocks to fulfill different goals. Both are decentralized in nature - this means there is no government agency or central bank or any other public or private authority controlling them. Blockchains on both these platforms are created and managed by the members of the public through mathematical consensus techniques. Both have their native cryptocurrencies (bitcoin and Ether) which can be utilized in their respective networks. Also, both these cryptos are available for trading and investing. For the last five years, bitcoin has remained the most valued cryptocurrency while ETH has maintained its second position.

While the underlying technologies are similar, Bitcoin and Ethereum are different in their goals, applications, and ambitions.

Let's explore.

And, the many differences

Gavin Wood, one of the founders of Ethereum, once famously described it as *one computer for the entire planet.* It's quite common for Ethereum's founders, developers, and global community to describe it as a 'world computer'. Imagine you have access to a globally decentralized computer that allows you to use different applications (gaming, investing, trading, social networking, and many more) or build your own applications by writing a few lines of code. The added advantage of Ethereum is that there is no controlling authority behind this global computer - this means, there is no censorship and none can block your accessibility as long as you play by the rules.

Let's take another analogy to understand the core philosophy of Ethereum.

Imagine Ethereum as an app store like the ones we have on our iPhones or Android-based smartphones. These stores allow us to download and use millions of apps. Also, we can develop our own apps for other users. The only difference is that these app stores are centralized - companies like Apple or Google control them. Ethereum's app store is completely decentralized and runs on smart contracts. Anyone can access, build and launch apps and interact with other users by creating these smart contracts and abiding by the contract rules.

All these applications and activities are running at the top of the Ethereum blockchain while smart contracts ensure that the entire system runs like a well-oiled machine. A smart contract is like the programmed rule in an automated vending machine - it dispenses the chosen product as long as you insert the right amount of money and press the right key. No third party is involved in the transaction and all activities run smoothly as per programmed rules.

In stark contrast to Ethereum, Bitcoin is meant for a very specific function - precisely, acting as a peer-to-peer payment mechanism without requiring any bank or other intermediary. By using Bitcoin, you can send money directly to Bob rather than instructing your bank to debit your account, which in turn sends the money to Bob's bank to credit his account. So, Bitcoin is like a decentralized banking application, rather than an entire app store. You can use this application to send or receive money or keep your savings. Simple and nothing more.

Design and purpose

While blockchain is at the heart of both platforms, Bitcoin and Ethereum blockchains are designed differently to serve different purposes. The blockchain in Bitcoin records historical transactions (movement of bitcoin to and from different addresses). The Ethereum blockchain records transactions along with lines of codes and data. Developers can create smart contracts of their choice (like 'transfer ownership of asset A to Bob when $X is received') to create any application like building a trading platform, an online game, or even a completely decentralized company that runs on codes. The possibilities are endless because Ethereum is Turing-complete (this means it's fully programmable to develop any application). Users need to pay a transaction fee to use these applications. These fees, paid in ETH, go to the validators of the Ethereum blockchain, who record these transactions in blocks and run the decentralized ledger.

Bitcoin is not Turing-complete. This means Bitcoin has very limited programmability and it cannot be modified to develop applications other than its specific purposes. Bitcoin is based on the simpler C++ programming language and has less than 70 specific commands. This limitation is intentional to keep the Bitcoin payment system secure and less vulnerable to exploitation. However, it also means Bitcoin can not be molded to suit a new application. According to Buterin, *Bitcoin is great as a form of •igital money, but its scripting language is too weak for any kin• of serious a•vance• applications to be built on top.* Bitcoin can work as a medium of exchange and store of economic value whereas Ethereum acts as a general-purpose blockchain. Or in Gavin Wood's words, Bitcoin is like email while Ethereum is like the entire Internet!

Consensus mechanism - PoW vs PoS

A decentralized blockchain needs a consensus mechanism to ensure all peers agree on the authenticity of the transactions recorded in blocks. This mechanism also guarantees that no single entity can control the blockchain and only true events get recorded. Bitcoin and Ethereum use two different consensus mechanisms. The former uses the more common Proof of Work (PoW) while the latter uses the relatively new Proof of Stake (PoS) mechanism.

PoW, as the name suggests, is a piece of evidence that a participant has done a certain amount of computing work. More specifically, this computing work involves solving increasingly complex mathematical puzzles. Users who can solve these puzzles are given a chance to build the next block in a probabilistic manner. As a reward, the chosen user receives a certain amount of bitcoin. This reward acts as an incentive for people to participate in building and maintaining the blockchain by investing their time and computing resources.

Even though PoW is the most established consensus mechanism, it requires specialized hardware like Application-Specific Integrated Circuit (ASIC) to solve these puzzles. Simply stated, PoW is a competition based on computing power. So as the puzzles get more complex and the number of transactions of Bitcoin rises, the electricity consumption of Bitcoin also rises, rapidly. In 2022 alone, Bitcoin consumed 107.65 terawatt-hours (TWh) of electricity - higher than that of the Philippines and 7 times more than the energy needs of Google's entire global operations. A large share of this energy comes from highly polluting energy sources like coal. A recent study by the University of Cambridge shows that Bitcoin transactions have caused a cumulative emission of 200 million tonnes of carbon dioxide since its launch. This figure was estimated to be 22-22.9 million metric tons in 2022 alone - surpassing the emission level of countries like Sri Lanka and Jordan. Such a gigantic energy requirement and the resulting environmental impacts put serious questions on Bitcoin's long-term sustainability.

PoS, on the other hand, relies on a staking system in which users need to stake a certain amount of ETH to participate in the race of completing blocks. The higher the ETH stake, the greater the probability that a particular participant gets a chance to complete a block. On completion, the participant gets transaction fees in ETH. The ETH stake ensures that no 'bad actor' can record false information or exploit the blockchain in any way as they have a stake to lose. So, it's a competition based on how much economic value one can put at stake. PoS doesn't need humongous computing power - one just needs ETH to stake. As we have mentioned initially, Ethereum's shift to PoS has lowered its energy consumption by 99.98%.

Supply

Bitcoin has an absolute supply cap of 21 million bitcoins. This means there cannot be any more new bitcoin in circulation once the 21 million ceiling is reached. bitcoin is designed to reach this magic number by halving the block reward every 4 years. Currently, there are more than 19 million bitcoin in circulation. Because of the halving process, bitcoin's supply cap of 21 million will be reached by the year 2140, when the last block award will be released. Proponents of bitcoin consider it a digital gold because of this supply cap. They expect Bitcoin, similar to physical gold, would hold its value in inflationary times.

Ethereum does not have a hard supply cap. Rather, its issuance rate is designed to fall over time. Initially, the issuance rate was 5 ETH per block, which fell to 3 ETH and then to the current issuance rate of 2 ETH per block. This means when a new block is created, 2 more ETH is released in circulation. After the completion of the current upgrades (which will lead to Ethereum 2.0), the issuance rate would fall to 1% per annum. So, every year the total Ethereum supply is expected to rise by 1% of the total ETH already in supply. This low supply growth would not have any significant inflationary pressure as long as the Ethereum ecosystem grows at a faster rate. Rather, if the Ethereum economy grows faster than the ETH supply growth, the value of ETH will keep increasing.

Throughput and scalability

Guess what - Ethereum is not only infinitely more energy efficient than Bitcoin, but it's also faster. Bitcoin currently processes 7 transactions per second on average while Ethereum processes 30. According to Vitalik Buterin, Ethereum's throughput (the number of transactions per unit of time) would rise to 100,000 transactions per second once the ongoing upgrades of the network are complete. Compare this to global payment processing giant Visa's current capacity of 24,000 transactions per second. Ethereum's faster transaction capacity would give it increased scalability compared to Bitcoin, which is unlikely to have further network upgrades. So, the Ethereum network is expected to expand at a higher rate in the future.

Can Ethereum be the one crypto to rule them all?

For one moment, let's forget about all the technical jargon like blockchain, peer-to-peer, and consensus mechanisms to think about the fundamentals. What determines the future potential of new technology? The precise answer is the economic value the technology would create. Economic value comes from applications and the adoption of technology. Bitcoin is designed to be a digital currency and its ultimate success would be to replace the dollar or to replace all global currencies to become the de facto global medium of exchange. We have already seen instances in which Bitcoin is filling the gap where traditional banking and monetary system is inefficient. For example, in September 2021, El Salvador became the first country to adopt bitcoin as a legal tender. One of the reasons behind this step was to lower the transaction costs of remittance payments from Salvadorans living abroad. However, replacing the dollar is quite far in the future given that the value of all bitcoins in the world is less than 1.5% of the total money supply in the world. Moreover, the high volatility is a colossal challenge for Bitcoin in the way of being accepted as either a reliable store of value or a medium of exchange.

In contrast, Ethereum has a blue ocean to explore. It's powering new business models like Decentralized Finance (DeFi), innovative modern-day organizations like Decentralized Autonomous Organizations (DAOs), and previously unheard-of asset classes like the Non-Fungible Tokens (NFTs). According to a report by JP Morgan, Ethereum runs more than 70% of DeFi applications. Also, Ethereum has ETH as its own medium of exchange and store of value to counter Bitcoin. If bitcoin is digital gold, Ethereum is the digital oil that can run the global economy.

So if we compare Ethereum with the app store and Bitcoin with a particular app, the app store always has a greater chance of survival than the particular app on it. Having said that, both these platforms can co-exist and thrive when each focuses on its individual strength - Bitcoin on decentralized payment and Ethereum on decentralized business applications.

Let's now look at how Ethereum is uniquely positioned to create value for investors.

Chapter 04

ETHEREUM'S COMPETITIVE MOAT - HOW THE NO.2 CRYPTO IS UNIQUELY POSITIONED IN THE MARKET

No formula in finance tells you that the moat is 28 feet wide and 16 feet deep. That's what drives the academics crazy. They can compute standard deviations and betas, but they can't understand moats.
- *Warren Buffett.*

In 1983, American engineer and entrepreneur Robert Metcalfe was delivering a presentation to his sales team at 3Com, the company he co-founded. During the address, he demonstrated one of his interesting observations on the utility of a growing network. Metcalfe, who earlier invented Ethernet (a fundamental networking technology, unrelated to Ethereum), showed that the economic value of a network grows in proportion to the square of the number of connected users. To state it simply - when the number of users in a network (like a crypto platform) grows from 10 to 11, the total economic value rises from 100 to 121. This observation, which later came to be commonly known as Metcalfe's law, explains how companies like Facebook, Google, Amazon, and Uber grew exponentially in a short period to assume near-monopoly status.

Since the 1980s, Metcalfe's law has been propagated extensively and applied to a wide range of situations. In economics, an implication of Metcalfe's law is the network effect. Minus the technical jargon, it means the total utility or value created by a platform rises rapidly as more users join it. As new users become part of a system, they all bring economic value to it, which in turn gets multiplied through their interactions to create an even larger overall value. For example, as more users join Tinder, there is a greater chance for everyone else on the platform to get their preferred matches. When each user derives more utility, the overall system creates a much greater level of value. Similarly, as more drivers register with Uber, customers would be able to book a ride faster from any location. This would attract more customers to Uber, which in turn would generate more revenue for the drivers. So, the overall value generated by the platform would rise exponentially.

Now, let's look at how the network effect is at play on the Ethereum network.

How Ethereum is Creating Value

Ethereum, with a growing community of developers, users, and investors is in a unique position to benefit from the network effect. As the number of participants in the Ethereum economy rises steadily, it can exponentially create economic value for all. Furthermore, Ethereum's unique value proposition - the ability to maintain a sustainable competitive advantage over its rivals - is the primary source of its economic moat. We can observe a confluence of several positive factors that are creating a competitive moat for Ethereum.

Let's look at those.

First mover advantage

July 16, 1995, an ambitious young man from Bellevue, Washington started an online bookstore - the first of its kind. Not many were convinced by the idea of selling books on the Internet. However, from being the first mover in a new industry, Jeff Bezos' Amazon grew to become the largest online retailer of today with $513.98 billion of annual revenue. It entered a small industry segment (books) first and then expanded its experience and learning to include a large portfolio of products (thus the moniker 'everything store') to serve the global market. The idea to take home - Amazon was hugely successful in exploiting its first-mover advantage.

When a company or a platform is the first one to enter an industry, it has more time to gain and accumulate technical knowledge than late entrants. It also has the first access to the talent pool - developers, contributors, and innovators. Finally, the first mover can build an early base of customers and users who would later find it more troublesome to switch from an established player to a new entrant. From Coca-Cola in soft drinks to Gillette in safety razors, Sony in personal stereos, and Uber in ride-sharing - there is no dearth of examples of the first mover advantage. It's the competitive edge that a firm receives by entering the market before anyone else.

Even though Ethereum is not the first cryptocurrency, it's the first player in the blockchain marketplace. Ethereum is the pioneer of the concept that an open blockchain platform can be used by developers to build all sorts of applications through a smart contract. Being first in the blockchain marketplace made it easier for Ethereum to create sufficient media hype, build a strong brand name, have a solid base of users and developers, accumulate technical know-how, and move a long distance along the learning curve. Even though in the last couple of years several competitors (most notably Solana, Cardano, Polkadot, and Avalanche) have entered the market to eat Ethereum's market share, Ethereum has maintained and indeed solidified its position in the smart contract space.

Let's look at the statistics.

As of April 2023, Ethereum commands about one-fifth of the entire crypto market valuation. According to a study by Zion Market Research, in 2022 the global smart contract market was valued at $1.75 billion of which Ethereum accounted for more than 43%. A January 2023 report by blockchain software company Alchemy shows that the number of smart contracts deployed on the Ethereum mainnet has grown by an astounding 293% from 2021.

If we look at Ethereum's daily verified contracts chart, we can see long-term secular growth in verified contracts, which is steadily inching toward 1,000 per day.

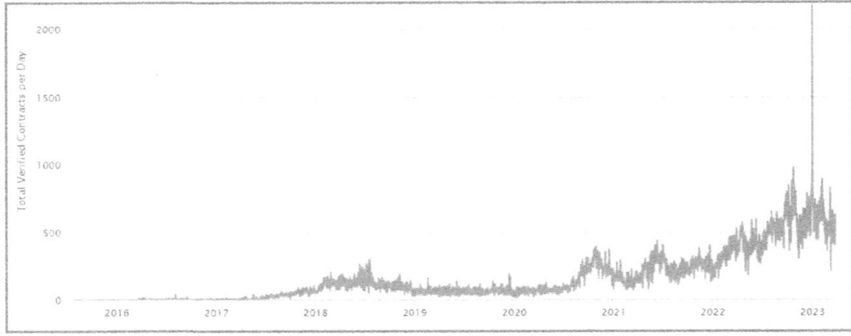

Figure 2: *Ethereum's daily verified contracts (Source: etherscan.io)*

Now, let's look at the Non-Fungible Token (NFT) sales figures. NFTs are smart-contract-based tokens that represent ownership of digital assets like a piece of art or music. When it comes to NFTs, Ethereum has a near-monopoly. According to CryptoSlam, Ethereum's all-time NFT sales figure is $29 billion compared to $4 billion sales by the second biggest NFT seller Ronin (RON).

These numbers show how Ethereum has reaped the first mover advantage to solidify its market position.

A booming community of developers and users

When it comes to the number of developers and users, Ethereum is the uncontested leader of the pack. According to a January 2022 report by Electric Capital, a crypto-centric venture capital firm, between 2018 and 2022, the number of monthly active Ethereum developers increased from 1,089 to 5,819 – an almost 5.5X growth! The report also states that Ethereum accounts for more than 16% of all crypto developers. More interestingly, while the crypto market faced a brutal bear market in 2022, Ethereum's developer count rose by 9% compared to an increase of 5% in the overall number of crypto developers. Quite evidently, Ethereum's Merge, its latest upgrade, was the most important crypto event of the year, which attracted a lot of new developers to the platform. Moreover, Ethereum's well-developed guidelines and token standards make it a great platform for developers. As of December 2022, Ethereum has 1,873 active full-time developers – greater than the total number of developers of the next 3 contenders combined – Polkadot (752), Cosmos (511), and Solana (383).

The user base on the Ethereum platform is also on a constant rise. According to Cryptonews, the number of Ethereum addresses holding a non-zero balance reached an all-time high of 92.5 million in January 2023. This figure was around 71 million at the end of 2021. This means that in 2 years there was a more than 30% growth in addresses holding some amount of Ethereum. In comparison, there are only 44 million addresses with non-zero balances on the Bitcoin network. The number of wallets with a positive balance is a proxy count for the volume of users on a blockchain platform.

A steady growth cafén the number of caférs and users means there would be a greater number of activities on the Ethereum platform. More developers translate into the creation and deployment of more applications, which in turn creates more value for users. As more users jump in, there would be more exchanges and collaborations on Ethereum. When there are more applications and activities, there will be greater demand for Ether (ETH), which will lead to its price appreciation. When ETH's value goes up, there would be more investors, which in turn would attract more developers and then more users. This cycle would continue for the long term, creating a network effect for Ethereum – benefiting all stakeholders.

- **A record of continuous improvement**

Since its inception, Ethereum has gone through several upgrades to become more scalable, secure, and sustainable without compromising on centralization. For example, the upgrade from Proof-of-Work (PoW) to Proof-of-Stake (PoS) made the network extremely energy efficient. The upcoming upgrades, which would include Layer 2 implementation and sharding (more on these in the next chapter), are expected to increase its throughput (no. of transactions per second) making Ethereum more scalable and secure. Every round of improvement and innovation makes the network more efficient and gives it an incremental competitive edge. As Ethereum continuously gets rid of the issues plaguing its performance, there would be less leeway for rivals to eat its market share.

Does Ethereum have an economic moat?

An economic moat is not anything tangible or directly identifiable; yet, it separates long-term value creators from others. When a company has an economic moat, it enjoys a certain long-term advantage over its competitors because its value creation process can't be easily imitated. For example, the economic moat of Apple makes it such a formidable player in the market – it has superior technology, a great talent pool, the capability to innovate continuously– a well-established brand equity, and a loyal customer base.

It turns out that Ethereum's first move– advantage, booming developer and user base, technological expertise, and the capability to improve continuously can create an economic moat for investors. As mentioned before, even though several competitors are trying to imitate

Ethereum's model, its market dominance remains unchallenged. As Ethereum scales up its capacity and makes the network more secure through several upgrades planned in the near future, Ethereum's economic moat will be more pronounced.

Let's now look at how the Ethereum network has improved over time through several upgrades and how it plans to lead ahead.

Chapter 05

THE ROAD TO EXCELLENCE – AN OVERVIEW OF ETHEREUM'S UPGRADES

You've got to start with the customer experience and work back toward the technology – not the other way around.
– Steve Jobs

2021 – somewhere in Argentina – Vitalik Buterin was trying to pay for tea using Ether (ETH) in a local café. But, to his surprise, the payment failed. The gas price (transaction fees on Ethereum) for the transaction was much higher than the upper limit set by him. So, he tried again with a higher gas price. Guess what – the payment failed the second time too. Now a glitch in the User Interface (UI) of his ETH wallet made it impossible to set a higher gas limit. This was not the first time Buterin had a reality check on the shortcomings of the 'world computer' he was trying to build.

A number of personal experiences like this made Buterin realize the challenges hindering the mass adoption of Ethereum. In his own words – *along with the all-important issue of high transaction fees due to scaling not yet been fully solved, user experience is a key reason why many Ethereum users, especially in the Global South, often opt for centralized solutions instead of on-chain decentralized alternatives...* User experience is a key element behind the success of any novel technology. Apple's legendary founder Steve Jobs had a staunch focus on prioritizing user experience above everything else. Buterin took a leaf out of Jobs' books and started focusing on enhancing user experience early on.

User experience is a result of multiple factors such as transaction speed, wait time, fees, security, and the level of control users have. Moreover, energy efficiency and environmental impact are other aspects that ensure a platform will be in business for the long term. These underlying elements affecting user experience fall under four broad categories – sustainability, scalability, security, and decentralization. As discussed before, Ethereum's shift from Proof-of-Work (PoW) to Proof-of-Stake (PoS) solved the sustainability problem by cutting its energy consumption by 99.9%.

Now, the last three, to a great extent, remain to be addressed.

Solving the blockchain trilemma in the Ethereum way

Global payment giant Visa can process up to 24,000 transactions in a second. So why does Ethereum process only up to 30 transactions per second?

The difference lies in centralization.

Visa's operations are centralized – this means you have limited control and privacy. You need to trust Visa that your money and personal information are safe with them. However, credit card frauds and data breaches are not rare. A 2023 report by security.org shows that in 2022, more than 65% of cardholders have been victims of credit card frauds of one or another type in their lifetime.

Transactions in a decentralized blockchain like Ethereum are verified and recorded by millions of nodes (network participants), which takes significant time. Scalability can be greatly increased by making a platform more centralized or by cutting the corners of its security infrastructure. For example, Solana (SOL) claims to execute up to 50,000 transactions per second, which comes via a big-time compromise on decentralization. Today, while Ethereum has around 500,000 validators, Solana has little more than 3,000. The higher the number of validators, the higher the level of decentralization – and the more users are in control of their money and personal data.

Security and empowerment of users through decentralization are two fundamental promises of blockchain. However, a blockchain platform can achieve mass adoption only when it's scalable – it can manage a large volume of transactions in real-time. This leads to the classical blockchain trilemma – apparently, it's very difficult to achieve security, scalability, and decentralization at the same time.

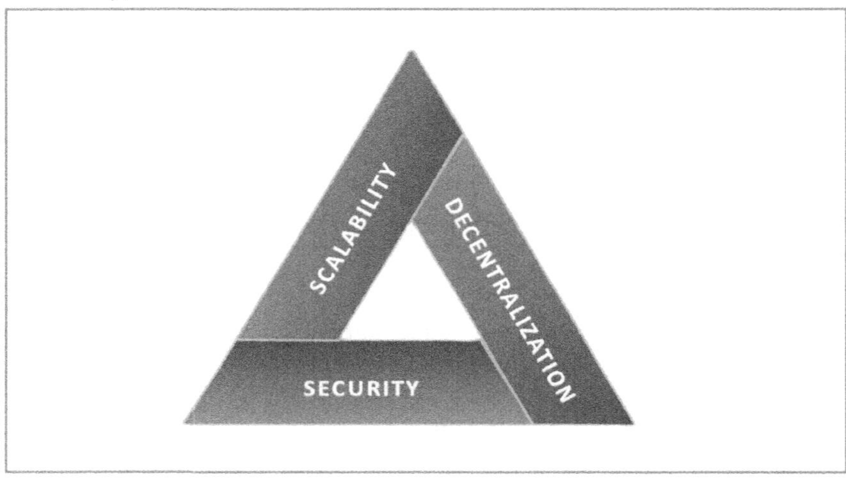

Figure 3: *Blockchain trillema (Source: ragonchain.com)*

Blockchain trilemma is not a new problem. It turns out that Ethereum's core team always had a long-term vision to solve this trilemma through innovation. According to Ethereum.org - *Ethereum's vision is to be more scalable an secure but also to remain ecentralize.* Ethereum has been relentlessly working on this vision for the last 8 years. During this period, the platform has gone through more than 10 upgrades, some of which are still in process (as of this books print). For example, the Byzantium upgrade in 2017 reduced block reward from 5 to 3 ETH (thereby reducing ETH's supply growth), the Istanbul upgrade in 2019 optimized gas cost and improved smart contracts while the Paris upgrade (also called the 'Merge') shifted its consensus mechanism from PoW to PoS making it a sustainable platform.

Put together, all these upgrades were earlier referred to by the umbrella term 'Ethereum 2.0 or Eth2'. Some of these upgrades resulted in forks (changes in the core Ethereum protocol) which led to temporary splits in the blockchain reflecting that the platform has now taken a more efficient route. For example, the Dao fork in 2016 was done to secure the network against the Dao attack that was discussed earlier in the book.

In a centralized system, like Visa, upgrades, and improvements are implemented top-down. Strategists at the senior level come up with a future roadmap, which in turn is communicated to the lower managerial levels for implementation. What about a decentralized system like Ethereum? How do a large community of developers and validators come to a consensus on a future roadmap? Let's see.

Ethereum Improvement Proposals (EIPs)

Monday, July 2, 2018, at the height of the 2017/18 crypto bull market, Ethereum users spent 5,862 ETH (worth around $2.7 million) in transaction fees. A bull market attracts more investors, users, and developers which leads to a surge in the number of transactions. Back then, the gas price dynamically went up with a rise in the transaction volume. As more people wanted to get their transactions recorded in the next block, they bid up the transaction cost. Users had to shell out as much as $5.70 for a single transaction, much higher than Buterin's long-held target of 5 cents per transaction. Moreover, an auction-based gas price meant there was no predictability about how much the next transaction is going to cost. So Buterin suggested an upgrade in the platform to increase block sizes to reduce congestion and make gas prices more predictable.

These types of suggestions to change any aspect of Ethereum's operations are formally called Ethereum Improvement Proposals (EIPs). Upgrades and changes in Ethereum are the results of proposals, debates, discussions, and the adoption of accepted suggestions. These proposals are formally documented through EIPs. An EIP contains all technical specifications of the upgrade and serves as the single 'source of truth' for the Ethereum community. Any community member can suggest a change or improvement through EIPs, which are identified by a sequence number. For example, Buterin's suggestion discussed above is known as EIP 1559.

All EIPs received from the community members are reviewed by a team of technical experts called EIP editors. The accepted EIPs are then forwarded for further discussion, improvement, and subsequent adoption by the community. Therefore, every network upgrade on Ethereum originates from EIPs which come from the larger Ethereum community. EIP 1559 was eventually implemented on August 5, 2021, through the London hard fork. Initially, the London upgrade was successful in lowering Ethereum's transaction cost and time. However, it was not sufficient.

It was time to implement more drastic changes to scale up the platform.

Beacon chain and the Merge

September 6, 2022, Forbes' digital edition came with the headline - *First Phase Of Ethereum Merge, Biggest Thing In Crypto Since Bitcoin, Goes Live.* After 9 days, Ethereum's Paris upgrade, more commonly known as the 'Merge' was fully implemented, opening a new chapter in the history of blockchain. Why was it considered such a significant event making big headlines?

The short answer is that the Merge addressed the biggest concern of the opponent of blockchain technology - its sheer environmental impact. The upgrade proved that it was possible to have a large-scale 'green crypto' platform with very low energy consumption and environmental impact. But why is the upgrade called 'Merge' in the first place?

Let's rewind a few years.

As we talked about before, scalability, security, and sustainability were always the core focus of Ethereum. But not everything can be achieved through a single step. Trying to augment scalability before addressing sustainability is quite like putting the cart before the horse. Therefore, Ethereum's first focus was to make the platform energy efficient by shifting its consensus protocol. But there is no single magic lever which the platform's fundamental protocol could pull to effect change. The merge was technologically complex - the reason its implementation got delayed by years after being originally conceived as early as 2014.

Think of Ethereum's shift from PoW to PoS as a train's shift from an inefficient fuel-guzzling engine to a super-efficient new one. However, before attaching the new engine to a running train, we must ensure that the engine is running as expected. There needs to be a trial run for the engine. Similarly, the PoS mechanism went through a trial run in the form of the Beacon chain starting in 2020. It was a separate blockchain running on PoS in parallel to the original Ethereum blockchain (also called Ethereum mainnet). Once the trial run was complete, the new engine was ready to get attached to the train.

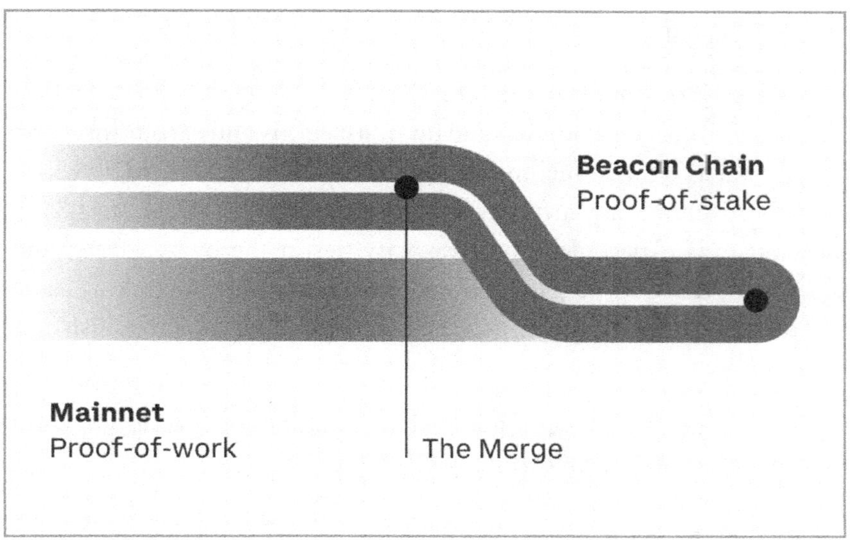

Figure 4: *The Merge (Source: Coinbase)*

'The Merge' signifies the merging of the Beacon chain with the Ethereum Mainnet, which shifted the consensus protocol. The result - one checkbox ticked - the question of sustainability was addressed.

As Ethereum is now a 'clean technology', it's expected to attract more attention from institutional investors for whom the environmental impact of blockchain was a red flag. According to Bank of America's analysts Alkesh Shah and Andrew Moss - *the significant reduction in energy consumption post-Merge may enable some institutional investors to purchase the token that [they] were previously prohibited from purchasing - tokens that run on blockchains leveraging proof-of-work (PoW) consensus mechanisms.*

The Merge also has a deflationary effect by lowering the rate of ETH issuance through reduced block rewards. Post Merge, the ETH issuance rate fell by around 90% from about 13,000 ETH/day to an average of 1,600 ETH/day. In October 2022, Ethereum became deflationary for the first time with the total supply of ETH falling marginally as more coins were burned than created. Note that a certain amount of ETH is 'burned' (put out of circulation) each time a transaction is validated and recorded in a block.

The Merge introduced staking of ETH to validate transactions. Stakers can lock ETH for a period to validate transactions and earn transaction fees as well as interest income (annual percentage yield or APY, which is currently hovering around 5%) on the staked ETH. The staking mechanism is expected to increase activities in the overall Ethereum ecosystem. Putting together the deflationary effects, staking, and greater institutional investment, the Merge presents a solid bullish case for ETH.

Moreover, the Merge was a major steppingstone for further upgrades to achieve a more scalable avatar of Ethereum.

The road ahead - more scalability, security, and decentralization

The Merge resolved Ethereum's sustainability problem to a great extent. However, there is a long way to go in terms of increasing its transaction speed and lowering transaction costs. As of February 2023, the median cost per transaction on Ethereum was $2.36 - still quite high. The primary reason behind the higher transaction cost is low scalability. As more and more dApps are developed, smart contracts are deployed, and NFTs are minted, the gas price can surge rapidly in the future while choking the blockchain.

However, looks like Ethereum has a solid upgrade plan in place to address these challenges.

Shanghai upgrade

After the Merge, the Shanghai upgrade, planned for April 12, 2023, is the next big event in Ethereum. This upgrade is significant because it will allow users to withdraw their staked ETH. As mentioned earlier, the Merge introduced staking for validating transactions and earning rewards. However, the staked ETH could not be withdrawn . The Shanghai upgrade would allow ETH withdrawal, which would increase liquidity for users. More importantly, once it becomes easy to withdraw the staked ETH, there would be greater interest in staking and validating transactions, which can make the platform more secure. The Shanghai upgrade will take place with another upgrade called Capella (which also facilitates staking withdrawals) on the same day. Combined, these two upgrades are referred to as 'Shapella'.

Before this upgrade, Ethereum allowed only regular staking - staking for validating transactions to secure the network. However, these staked funds are locked for a certain period. So it creates a short-term disadvantage for stakers. This is a reason ETH currently has a very low staking ratio (the percentage of total ETH supply in stake) of 15% compared to 70%+ of Solana (SOL) and Cardano (ADA). However, the

Shapella upgrade would allow liquid staking. This means users would still be able to access their staked ETH through tokens. These tokens can be used to generate additional income as they can be deposited as collateral on different crypto exchanges.

There is quite a bullish anticipation regarding the Shapella upgrade. Prior to the big day, ETH was trading at the 8-month high price of around $1920 as of the first week of April 2023.

Sharding, layer 2 implementations, and the big plans

Ethereum's shift to the PoS consensus mechanism makes it possible to implement various scalability solutions. Sharding is one of the most promising technologies that can make Ethereum truly scalable. It will involve breaking the Ethereum network into smaller components called shards. Each shard will function independently with its own smart contract. These shards will parallelly process all transactions coming to the Ethereum blockchain, which can drastically improve Ethereum's throughput. Once the whole Ethereum blockchain is broken into smaller segments, each segment can validate only a subset of transactions rather than all the transactions on the blockchain. Instead of assigning a large group of people to execute a series of tasks, sharding involves making smaller sub-groups and allocating each subgroup a sub-set of tasks so that all tasks are processed in parallel. Clearly, sharding can help Ethereum process exponentially more transactions. However, sharding involves a number of technical challenges because of which its implementation is expected to be a bit bumpy. Ethereum plans to implement sharding sometime in 2023/24.

Similarly, layer 2 implementation is another solution to the scalability problem. Layer 2 will create a separate blockchain that will extend the Ethereum mainnet (Layer 1). Once layer 2 is implemented, layer 1 will be responsible for security, data availability, and decentralization while layer 2 will take care of scalability. We will discuss Layer 2 in great detail in Chapter 10.

Vitalik Buterin, Ethereum's celebrated founder, has laid down some other grand plans for the platform. In rhyme with the Merge, these future upgrades are named the Surge (addresses scalability), the Scourge (focuses on decentralization), the Verge (relates to validation of blocks), the Purge (focuses on reducing computational costs and simplifying the platform) and the Splurge (anything that doesn't fit other categories). Going forward, we will have greater clarity on how these poetically ambitious plans are put into action.

For now, let's look at some of the nitty-gritty of investing in cryptos for the first time.

Chapter 06

LEARNING TO SWIM IN UNCHARTED WATERS - GETTING INTO CRYPTOS FOR THE FIRST TIME

I coul• either watch it happen or be a part of it.
- Elon Musk

Turkish-born Iranian-American economist Nouriel Roubini is a straight talker. Time and again, he has absolutely written off any investment worthiness of cryptos. At the World Economic Forum in January 2023, he even went to the extent of saying - *you have to stay away [from crypto.] You have to absolutely stay* away. *Literally, 90% of crypto is a scam.* Roubini, a former economics professor at New York University, is not the first one to decry cryptos. Starting from Christine Lagarde, president of the European Central Bank, to the US Treasury Secretary Janet Yellen and the legendary investor Charlie Munger - there is no dearth of crypto critics. Yet, the technology has not only survived for around one and a half decades, being stress tested by at least 2 severe bear markets along the way, but also thrived to become a $1.2 trillion asset class.

Crypto is not merely a buzzword. It has some solid business cases and applications that can plug the loopholes of a centralized financial system. This is why crypto has an impressive list of loyalists - starting from the tech evangelist and the world's second richest man Elon Musk to financial commentator Jim Cramer, venture capitalist Tim Draper and the famous investment author Robert Kiyosaki. According to TripleA Global Crypto Ownership data, there are currently (as of April 2023) more than 420 million crypto users in the world. In addition to a large number of retail investors, crypto is increasingly being recognized as a preferred investment option by institutional investors. In May 2022, financial service giant JP Morgan announced that crypto has overtaken real estate as one of its preferred alternative assets. The same year, the world's largest asset management company Blackrock launched a Bitcoin Trust to facilitate crypto investment for its institutional clients. In December 2022, the world's second-largest investment bank Goldman Sachs committed to investing tens of millions of dollars in crypto firms to augment its crypto portfolio.

When the movers and shakers of the financial world are moving into cryptos, 'staying away' doesn't sound like a wise decision.

There is nothing new about innovative technology being severely criticized or even being written off in the initial years. Think of the Internet. The biggest invention of the last century had to go through its own share of pain before becoming the lifeline of today's society. Cryptos can ensure financial inclusion, ease cross-border payments, make financial transactions more secure, serve as a hedge against inflation, and, like in the case of Ethereum, run the next-generation Internet through new applications.

To cut a long story short, cryptos have a huge investment potential if you stick to the right ones and follow the basic rules of investing. A historical observation in investing is that a rising tide lifts all boats. The hype around cryptos gives an opportunity to fly-by-night companies to enter the market and dupe investors (more on this later in the book). A few bad players often give a bad reputation to the entire industry. But, you can save yourself from these Ponzi schemes if you follow the basic principles of investing. Since crypto is another asset class, all fundamental rules of investing – starting from due diligence to money management – are equally applicable here.

If you missed the first wave of investing in cryptos, don't worry. It's never too late to have a share of one of the most promising emerging asset classes.

Let's look at the essentials for a beginner in crypto investing.

First things first - knowing what you are getting into

Legendary value investor Peter Lynch once famously said - *know what you own an• know why you own it.* There is no shortcut to doing your due diligence before investing in any asset - be it stocks, bonds, currencies, gold, or cryptos. Ideally, you should enter the field of crypto only when you are convinced of its potential as a driver of the future economy. And what can be a greater source of conviction than knowledge?

At the time of writing this book, there are around 9,000 active cryptocurrencies in the world (some with amusing names like PutinCoin, BurgerCities, Dracula Token, and PancakeSwap). In comparison, the total number of publicly traded companies in the US is less than 4,500. Different cryptos have different underlying technologies, visions, business models, and value drivers. It's easy to get overwhelmed, lost, and eventually demotivated if you try to get hold of each of them.

An ideal starting point is to get familiar with the underlying technology behind cryptos in general and then focus on some of the leading names. Next, you can dig deeper into their applications and value propositions. You need to ask how a particular crypto platform is going to create value. Bitcoin's value comes from its success as a digital currency. Similarly, Ethereum derives its value from the decentralized economy (DeFi, dApps, DAOs, and NFTs) it's going to run. There is no fundamental reason to invest in a crypto platform if its value-creation model is not clearly defined and understood. Afterall an asset becomes valuable only when it creates value in the real economy. A company's stocks do well in the market when its products and services create value in the real economy. So the return from any crypto investment eventually boils down to its real value creation.

In addition to the business model, you need to explore some other aspects like who are the founders, what is their vision, what are the performance indicators (like market cap, energy efficiency, scalability, no. of users and developers, uptime vs. downtime, and security breaches if any), and how transparent is the platform. Bogus crypto platforms, Ponzi schemes, and scams (more on these on Chapter 11) are not uncommon in the world of cryptos.

A good starting point is to focus on the top 10 crypto platforms in terms of market cap. This is because the market cap reflects how much the overall market is pricing a particular platform. Towards the end of this book, we will discuss what an ideal crypto portfolio should look like.

Once you have done your homework and you have a list of cryptos to invest in, the next step is to sign up with the right crypto exchange.

Finding the right crypto exchange

By July 2021, FTX, founded in May 2019, became the third-largest crypto exchange in the world with over 1 million users. Then, in less than one and a half years, the exchange filed for bankruptcy following the revelation of a major scam that wiped out more than $8 billion of its customers' money. FTX's fall from grace was really quick, shaking the confidence of common investors on crypto exchanges.

Crypto exchanges, the platforms on which you can buy and sell cryptos, are your gateways to the exciting world of crypto investing. An exchange allows you to buy cryptos using fiat money (like the dollar), exchange one crypto for another, and sell cryptos. An ideal crypto exchange is easy to use, lays down its terms loud and clear, and supports a variety of coins to choose from. According to the crypto news platform Cryptimi, currently, there are more than 500 crypto exchanges. Here again, our advice is to stick to the most reputed, established, and transparent ones.

Some of the most important factors for evaluating crypto exchanges are - years of operation, no. of users, no. of cryptos being offered, user interface, trading fees, transparency (how easy it is to find information), regulation status, reputation, customer support, technical support (charts, trading platforms, and trade signals), ease of deposit and withdrawals, and security. Since the number of factors is large, you need to put some time into evaluating the leading exchanges before settling for one. An established and reputed exchange with a large number of retail and institutional users can provide more security to your funds than a new entrant.

Going by the above-mentioned factors, Coinbase is one of the leading crypto exchanges today. Founded in 2012 by Brian Armstrong, a prominent flag bearer of the crypto industry, Coinbase is itself a publicly traded company and a part of the prestigious NASDAQ index. Coinbase has 110 million+ users out of which around 14,500 are institutional clients like banks and hedge funds. It supports more than 250 cryptos. Kraken is another user-friendly, innovative, and low-cost crypto exchange suitable for beginners. Founded in 2011, Kraken is one of the pioneers of crypto trading. It currently offers 185 cryptos including all the major ones. Opening an account on these exchanges is quite easy and straightforward. You can use a variety of payment options to buy cryptos. Similarly, you can transfer your funds to your bank accounts once you have sold your cryptos.

Keeping your cryptos safe

Tuesday, August 2, 2022, more than 8,000 users of a Solana-based crypto wallet saw their cryptos being siphoned off by hackers. Further investigation found that the security breach, which put an $8 million dent in investors' funds, took place on a mobile application named 'Slope Wallet'. While crypto platforms and exchanges are trying to implement the best technological solutions to protect investors, hackers and scammers often get ahead in the race. Crypto exchange Liquid Global was hacked in 2021 in which cryptos worth $97 million were lost. In 2022, $30 million worth of cryptos was stolen from the crypto exchange crypto.com. According to software security firm Immunefi, investors lost cryptos worth $12 billion in 2021 and 2022 through various instances of theft and scams. While there is nothing very difficult in buying and selling cryptos or exchanging one crypto for another, you need to put some extra care to keep your cryptos safe.

Let's look into some technical details to get a better idea on how to protect your cryptos from theft. Cryptos work on cryptographic encryption - a digital technique to keep information secret. Commonly, cryptos use a technique called asymmetric cryptography which involves a public and a private key. The public key is like an address, which allows you to receive a transaction (like receiving a certain amount of ETH) and the private key allows you to send a transaction (like sending ETH to someone). The public key is more like your email address which you need to give to others to receive emails. The private key is like the password of your email account, without which you cannot access or send emails to others. The private key is your secret key as it allows you to establish your ownership of your cryptos or use it for payment. This is the most important tip: never share your private key with anyone. Most crypto thefts and scams take place when a hacker gets access to your private keys in one way or the other (like sending malware to your computer).

When you buy cryptos through exchanges, you are provided with a crypto wallet that contains your private and public keys. Here, basically you don't control your private key. Rather, your private key is in the custody of the exchange. It's like keeping your gold in a bank's vault trusting its security. This is the reason these types of crypto wallets are called custodial wallets. If you are using a custodial wallet, which is the most convenient practice, ensure you have two-factor authentication. This type of authentication gives an extra layer of security to your crypto wallet. A common two-factor authentication is getting a One-Time Password (OTP) over your phone to authenticate transactions. So even if hackers have access to your crypto account, they cannot withdraw your cryptos unless they have the OTP as well.

Some exchanges like Coinbase provide self-custody crypto wallets. In these wallets, your private key is saved in your mobile and not with the exchange. So these wallets give you better control over your cryptos. However, as the saying goes - with great power comes great responsibility. Since the private key is in your own custody, you have no one to blame if you lose your private key and your cryptos.

In addition to these wallets discussed so far, there are hot wallets (Internet-based wallet applications) and cold wallets (hardware-based offline wallets). In both cases, you have custody of your own private key, which you need to keep safe. Chapter 11 of the book discusses in detail the common crypto scams and how you can keep your cryptos safe. Moreover, there are video tutorials regarding investing in cryptos for beginners that you can find on our website at: freemanpublications.com/bonus

Once you know what you are getting into and have a crypto account with an exchange, you are ready to explore the whole new world of cryptos. Remember that when it comes to investing in any asset, the time-tested investing rules are never out of favor. So be patient, don't follow the crowd, do your own analysis and stick to your convictions.

Let's now look at how we can determine the value of Ethereum from an investing point of view. Can the traditional fundamental analysis be of any use here?

Let's find out.

Chapter 07

HOW DO WE MEASURE ETHEREUM'S VALUE?

The secret to investing is to figure out
the value of something - and then pay a lot less.
*- **Joel Greenblatt,** American Investor, and Hedge Fund Manager.*

Samuel Langhorne Clemens, the famous American writer and humorist, commonly known by his pen name Mark Twain, was a man of wit. Though he is widely recognized for his literary works, it's a little-known fact that he significantly ventured, and burned his fingers, into financial investments. His early success in literary works brought him fame and a good amount of wealth, most of which was later squandered through reckless financial speculation in the stock market. So, the legendary author, with his characteristic wit, famously wrote - *October: this is one of the peculiarly dangerous months to speculate in stocks. The others are July, January, September, April, November, May, March, June, December, August, and February.*

Badly debt-ridden in his 60s, Mark Twain went back to writing books and lecturing in cities across the world. The money came pouring in again, making up for his lost fortune. Older and wiser - he ventured into stocks once more. But this time, not as an amateur speculator but as a seasoned value investor - keeping his money in the blue-chip stocks (companies with significant market power) of the day. All's well that ends well.

Speculation, no matter how enticing, is a sure-shot way to financial ruin. Speculative investing is all about following the crowd, looking for quick profits, chasing the 'hot' assets of the day, and taking excessive risks with complete disregard for sound investing principles. Value investing, on the other hand, is about managing risks, following proven investment rules, and focusing on long-term wealth creation.

A basic tenet of value investing is knowing the intrinsic value of an asset and then buying the asset when the market offers it at a significantly lower price. This gives a margin of safety because the price paid is much lower than the value received. It's easy to know the market price of an asset; but what about the intrinsic value? In the case of stocks, we commonly follow fundamental analysis to determine intrinsic value. Can we apply the same on Ethereum?

Let's find out.

Why the traditional fundamental analysis may not work for Ethereum

Fundamental analysis is based on looking into factors like the financial health of the company (capital structure, debt level, profit margin, revenue growth, and earnings per share), business model, market share, competition, and even the brand value. For example, higher debt indicates a lower intrinsic value for a stock whereas a high market share increases its intrinsic value. Fundamental analysis works perfectly well for publicly traded companies - all this information is easily available. But how do we measure things like the P/E ratio (ratio of share price and earnings per share) of Ethereum which does not have the structure of a traditional company?

Ethereum is more of a technological platform that facilitates economic activities. So measuring its intrinsic value needs a slightly different approach than the traditional fundamental analysis. Keeping the core concept of fundamental analysis (analyzing the value creation process) intact we can give it a twist to suit Ethereum's case. Rather than considering Ethereum as a company, we can look at it as a digital economy. The intrinsic value of Ether (ETH), Ethereum's digital currency, depends on the performance of the Ethereum economy. So, to get an idea of the fair value of ETH, we need to look at the factors affecting the performance of the 'Ethereum economy'.

Like in the real-world economy, the price of a certain commodity depends on the forces of demand and supply. When the demand is higher relative to supply, the price tends to go up. Conversely, when the demand is lower relative to supply, the price tends to fall. ETH's value, too, depends on its relative demand and supply in the Ethereum economy. Once we get to know the factors that influence ETH's demand and supply, we can have an idea about its fair price. In crypto jargon, the underplay of demand and supply of cryptos to determine its value is called tokenomics - token + economics. Tokenomics explains how cryptocurrencies become valuable assets for investing.

Determinants of Ethereum's value and price

If we look at ETH's price history, it traded under $1 for the most part of 2015 and crossed the $10 mark for the first time in March 2016. Then came the crypto bull market starting in 2017. ETH crossed $100 in May 2017 and ended the year at the peak price of $774.69 before crossing the $1,000 mark within a week into 2018! The crypto boom was followed by a huge crash. ETH was trading at around $100 a piece by the end of 2018 losing more than 90% of its value within a year.

The next 2 years were relatively stable with ETH trading in a narrow range. By the second half of 2020, ETH started appreciating again with a boom in the overall crypto market, rapid growth in Decentralized Finance (DeFi) and dApps, and an unprecedented increase in the global money supply. ETH reached a peak of $4,815 on November 9, 2021. Since then, it corrected significantly to about $1,100 by the mid- 2022. Starting from January 2023, ETH has been recovering steadily and is currently trading at around a 9-month high price of $1,898 (as of May 2023).

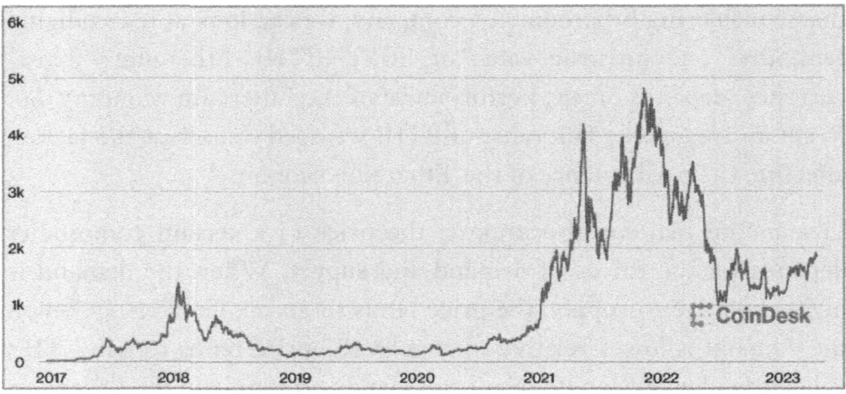

Figure 5: *ETH's price history (Source: coinmarketcap.com)*

Let's try to break down these price trends with the help of tokenomics.

Demand-side factors

In 2020, total value locked (total value of crypto assets staked in a platform) in the DeFi industry went up from $700 million to $15 billion - a whopping 2,100% increase. The same trend continued in dApps and the NFT space as well. The number of daily unique active wallets connected to dApps increased by 700% in 2021 to reach an all-time high of 2.7 million by the end of the year. We have seen a corresponding rise in ETH's price. So, where is the connection?

Since ETH is the currency of the Ethereum economy, users need to spend it every time they want to do a transaction (like creating a gaming app or using one) on the Ethereum blockchain. We have already mentioned how DeFi, dApps, and the NFT space are dominated by Ethereum. When there is growth in activities in these domains, the demand for ETH goes up and so does ETH's price. As more developers and users get on the Ethereum platform, the overall value of the Ethereum economy goes up because of the network effect we discussed earlier in the book. The network effect is self-reinforcing, and it creates a cycle of growth. Just as the demand for a country's currency rises with more economic activities and a higher GDP, the demand for ETH rises with more activities in the Ethereum ecosystem. So if you want to have an idea about ETH's value or expected price moves, you need to look at the on-chain metrics - data related to activities on the Ethereum blockchain such as number of smart contracts executed, the number of active wallets and the total value locked. You can get access to such on-chain data from Ethereum's official website, crypto news websites (like CoinDesk and Decrypt), or on-chain analytics providers like Glassnode.

Some of the other factors that can increase demand for ETH are staking and investment demand. Users can earn rewards by staking their ETH and validating transactions on the Ethereum blockchain. Since staking opens a new avenue of income for validators, it creates additional demand for ETH. Moreover, an overall boom in the crypto market brings more investors to cryptos. Ethereum's number 2 position in the market would create significant demand for ETH at times of market booms.

Lastly, as newer crypto assets like meme coins are created and traded, there will be additional demand for ETH. Meme coins are generally developed based on Internet memes. They are mainly created for fun. However, highly popular meme coins like Dogecoin (DOGE) and Shiba Inu (SHIB), can have speculative values for traders. Meme coins are crypto tokens, many of which follow Ethereum's token standards. For example, the highly popular Shiba Inu (SHIB) is based on Ethereum's token standard ERC-20. So the more these coins are created and traded, the higher ETH's demand would be. As of writing this book, an ongoing meme coin craze has been pushing Ethereum's usage to new heights.

Supply-side factors

Analyzing demand-side factors alone gives only half of the picture. Supply is the other half. Unlike Bitcoin, Ethereum's supply does not have a hard cap. However, it doesn't mean ETH's supply is unlimited. Ethereum has a monetary policy in place that aims to keep its supply stable. The relative strength of demand and supply determines ETH's scarcity and the direction of its price. What happens in the real economy when the money supply grows faster than the GDP? The value of money falls and there is inflation. The same rule applies to Ethereum. If the supply growth is faster than the demand growth, Ethereum will be inflationary- its value will go down. On the other hand, if the supply grows slower than demand, Ethereum will be deflationary - and its value will go up.

ETH's supply depends on two variables - the rate of issuance and the rate of burn. Under the Proof-of-Stake (PoS), new ETHs are issued and rewarded to stakers for validating transactions. These newly created ETHs put into circulation are the primary source of ETH's supply. The burning mechanism of ETH was introduced through the EIP-1559 in August 2021. This EIP simplified transaction fees by breaking the fees into two parts - base fee and tips (which users could provide to get their transactions recorded faster). Under the burning mechanism, the base fee is burnt (taken out of circulation), technically, this base fee, which is expressed as a certain amount of ETH is sent to a wallet without a private key. So, nobody can access it and it eventually goes out of supply. This base fee is dynamic - it expands when transaction volume is high and contracts when transaction volume is low. So when the network gets busy, more ETH is burned as the base fee goes up. The burning mechanism introduces a deflationary feature to the Ethereum economy.

Now, as you can see, the inflation or deflation rate of ETH depends on how much ETH is issued and how much is burnt in a given period. The issuance rate is a variable as it depends on the amount of ETH staked. Post Merge, the issuance rate fell drastically (around 90%) from around

13,000 ETH a day to about 1,700 ETH a day.

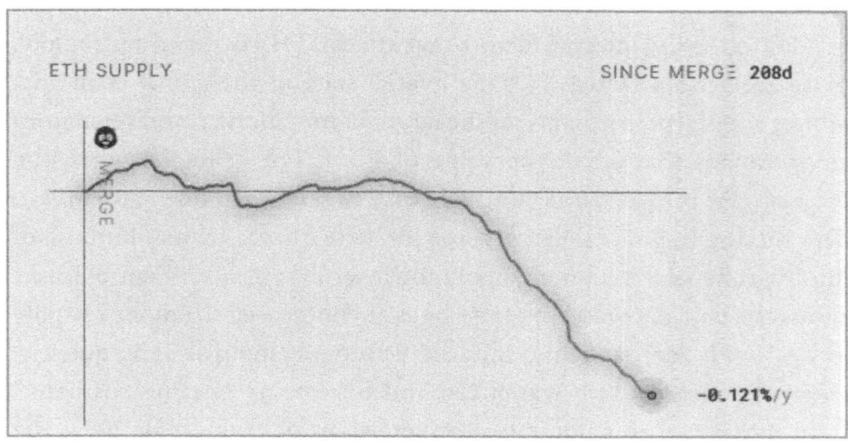

Figure 6: *ETH's Supply post-Merge (Source: ultrasound.money)*

The planned Shanghai upgrade will make it possible to withdraw staked ETH, which can potentially increase the staking ratio. A higher staking rate would increase ETH issuance (as more transactions will be validated in a given period). However, higher staking would also lock a portion of ETH lowering its free float (the amount of ETH available for trading in the market). Taken together, these can have a deflationary effect on ETH.

Combined, the burning mechanism and the Merge have been hugely successful in stabilizing ETH's supply. Between August 2021 (when the burn was introduced) and January 2023, about 2.8 million ETH worth around $4.6 billion have been removed from circulation through burning. The current supply of ETH is about 121 million, which is only 1.4% higher than one year ago. So, you can say that the Ethereum economy's current annual inflation rate is 1.4%. This is a low and stable rate compared to the US economy's current 6% inflation rate. As long as the Ethereum economy grows faster than the supply growth of ETH, the value of the latter is likely to appreciate.

Other factors

In addition to the internal factors that affect ETH's demand and supply, there are certain factors like the overall state of the global economy, money supply, performance of the larger crypto market, and regulatory environment that affect the value of ETH. For example, when the interest rate is lower, it is relatively easy to borrow money and invest. The soaring bull market in cryptos in 2020/21 was mainly because of this huge increase in money supply and low interest rates. Central banks across the world lowered interest rates and increased the money supply to deal with the pandemic-induced economic slumps. Subsequently, when the interest rate was hiked and borrowing became costlier, a large portion of this liquidity was taken out of cryptos. In 2022, the larger crypto market experienced a severe bear market in which both ETH and bitcoin went down by more than 75%. So, ETH's value is likely to go up in a low-interest-rate environment and go down in a high-interest-rate environment.

ETH's investment demand can also go up because of the deflationary effects post-Merge. Inflation in the larger economy leads to a fall in the dollar's purchasing power. In such a case, investors can find ETH to be a great hedging option against inflation. So, an inflationary economic environment, similar to the current global economic phase, can push up ETH's value through higher investment demand.

Ethereum's price also has a strong correlation with that of bitcoin. According to data from IntoTheBlock (ITB), ETH's correlation with bitcoin as of March 2023 was 0.98 - which is a near-perfect correlation. This means both cryptos show similar price movements. Moreover, ETH's price moves are in sync with the sentiment regarding the overall crypto market. Bitcoin, commanding around half of the total crypto market valuation, is still the uncontested numero uno. Its performance sends a signal to investors regarding the overall health of the crypto market. So it's not a surprise that no. 2 is closely correlated to no. 1.

Another important factor affecting ETH's relative valuation is market competition. A number of blockchain platforms like Solana (SOL), Cardano (ADA), Polkadot (DOT), and Avalanche (AVAX) are trying to make their presence felt in the blockchain marketplace. However, each of these platforms has its own challenges to deal with. For example, Solana (SOL) had multiple downtimes in 2022 and at the beginning of 2023. Ethereum, with its clear vision, strong market presence, and multiple upgrades, is in a great position to maintain its market dominance.

Finally, the changing regulatory environment can alter sentiments regarding investing in cryptos. While accommodative government policies can boost crypto's perceived value, stricter regulations can dampen investors' sentiment. An overall supportive regulatory environment can enhance Ethereum's value. However, Ethereum has a very positive case even if regulations become stricter (more on this in Chapter 13). Since Ethereum is a blockchain marketplace, it can find it easier to comply with stricter government regulations compared to special purpose blockchains like Bitcoin. After all, Ethereum has a blue ocean of applications to offer.

Let's now explore DeFi, arguably the most promising recent innovation in the financial industry.

Chapter 08

DECENTRALIZED FINANCE (DEFI) - TRADITIONAL FINANCE MEETS NEW-AGE SMART CONTRACTS

DeFi is what happens when you combine the power of crypto with the openness of the internet.
*– **Nick Szabo**, American Computer Scientist, an• Cryptographer.*

More than 60% of sub-Saharan Africans are small farmers. When they want to insure crops against adverse weather conditions, we expect them to go to traditional insurance companies. But, for most of the smallholder farmers in Africa, this is not a viable option. The African continent, home to about 17% of the world's population, has a very low insurance penetration - only around 2.78% as of 2022. In Africa, the barriers to getting crop insurance are high, the steps to get one are many, and the associated costs can be prohibitive. The result - there is no effective risk-mitigation mechanism for farmers, and they remain at the mercy of the volatile weather. Climate change is making things worse.

When the traditional financial system, which is centralized to the core, fails to reach such a large chunk of humanity, technological innovations can come to their rescue. Etherisc, a blockchain-based insurance company from Germany is doing just that. It has created a crop-insurance platform for parametric insurance that minimizes operational costs, fulfills the specific needs of small farmers, and automatically processes claims using smart contracts.

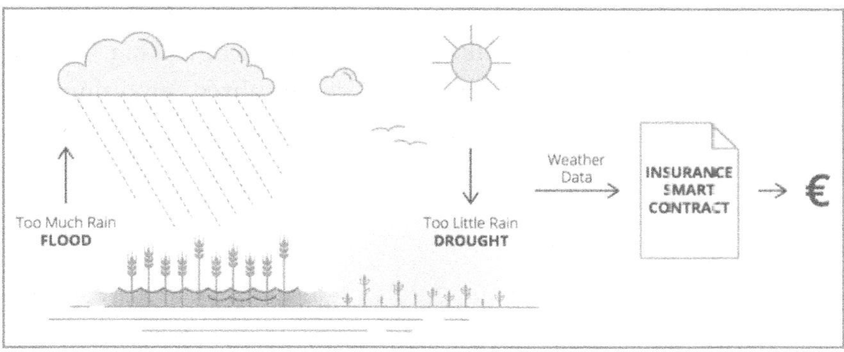

***Figure** 7: Parametric insurance (Source: Ethersic)*

Parametric insurance processes insurance claims on the basis of external parameters like weather conditions. Suppose a farmer buys insurance against an adverse weather event like a flood or drought. The smart contract defines what weather parameters (amount of rain, temperature, and precipitation) constitute an adverse climatic condition. Etherisc collects data from satellites and the smart contract automatically processes the insurance claims whenever these events occur. So, there is no need for filing time-consuming insurance applications, visiting the insurer's office, applying for claims, proving the extent of damage, and waiting for the claim to be processed (sometimes, this never happens when local laws are weak).

Since Ethersic has very low manpower requirements and all transactions happen on the blockchain through smart contracts, the operational cost is low. This means farmers need only to pay low premiums - sometimes as low as $0.50. Moreover, farmers can avail themselves of these insurance products using just a mobile app. By April 2022, more than 22,000 Kenyan farmers have availed of Ethersic's services. The problems of accessibility and affordability are greatly resolved through Ethersic's blockchain-based insurance products. Most interestingly, Ethersic's entire insurance platform is powered by Ethereum.

Ethersic is not the only firm using Ethereum's smart contracts to redefine the rules of finance. There are hundreds of other firms and platforms providing services like saving, insurance, trading, money transfer, and loans in a completely decentralized environment. Welcome to the world of Decentralized Finance (DeFi).

What is DeFi?

Brian Armstrong, CEO of Coinbase, said *DeFi is one of the most exciting developments in crypto and has the potential to revolutionize the financial system as we know it.* According to Ethereum's founder Vitalik Buterin, *DeFi is the future of finance.* If we go by the opinion of Harriet Taylor, Executive Director of the UN World Food Programme, *with DeFi, we can build a more inclusive financial system that works for everyone.* So, what is DeFi and why are these industry stalwarts so upbeat about it?

Take blockchain's decentralization, privacy, immutability, accessibility, and security and then apply them to real-world finance - what you get is DeFi. It's the application of the best things blockchain has to offer to revolutionize financial transactions. DeFi happens when Etherisc uses Ethereum's smart contract to take crop insurance to a large number of people, who earlier did not have access to traditional financial platforms. In this case, it's DeFi insurance. Similarly, think of a platform that allows you to borrow money instantly without the lengthy loan application process in a bank or the hassles of proving your creditworthiness. This is DeFi lending. And what about trading financial assets like stocks or derivative contracts with other peers across the world without going through a broker, paying high transaction costs, while having complete control over your funds? Here is your DeFi exchange.

But all these financial activities have been working fine even before the arrival of blockchain. So what is the big deal?

DeFi allows you to do everything that a traditional financial institution like a bank, an insurance company, or a security broker has to offer. However the unique value proposition is that DeFi makes all these transactions more efficient, secure, private, and trustless while giving you complete control over your finances. DeFi makes its services accessible through decentralized apps (dApps) which can be accessed by anyone with an Internet connection.

Think of stock trading - if you can buy from and sell stocks to other peers without having to register with a broker, locking your funds and securities with it and trusting it with your finances, you will save on transaction fees and get an instant settlement without revealing too much of your personal information or losing your sleep over the safety of your funds. Peer-to-peer financial transactions were not possible before blockchain, so we needed a trusted intermediary like a bank or a broker. Now, DeFi is not only feasible but also the future of finance - especially with Ethereum's smart contracts.

Today, DeFi is not only helping African small farmers access banking and insurance services, or Argentinians save themselves from crippling inflation, but also enabling millions of users to invest their savings, trade with others, borrow funds, manage portfolios, schedule payments, and much more. Centralized finance (CeFi) did all these at a huge cost to the users. DeFi is changing the face of finance. In 2022, DeFi was a $14.1 billion industry with Ethereum controlling about 60% of the market. According to InsightAce Analytic, the global DeFi market is expected to reach $398.77 billion by 2031 with a compound annual growth rate (CAGR) of 45.16%, putting a significant dent in CeFi.

How does DeFi differ from CeFi?

In March 2023, two giant US banks - Silicon Valley Bank (SVB) and Signature Bank - failed, making them the second and third largest bank failures respectively in US history. At the time of their failure, the total value of their combined assets was worth about $327 billion. The

Federal Deposit Insurance Corporation (FDIC) insures deposits only up to $250,000 for a single depositor. More than 86% of SVB's deposits were higher than this deposit insurance limit of FDIC. Depositors' money is hardly safe with the so-called safest of US banks.

According to FDIC data, between 1980 and 1995 more than 2,900 banks and thrifts (savings and loans providers) with assets over $2.2 trillion failed. The global financial crisis resulted in the failure of more than 500 US banks and financial institutions between 2007 and 2014. According to Pew Research, there have been more than 25 bank failures in the US between 2015 and 2022. When a bank fails, depositors, who trusted the banks with their money, are the main losers. A survey by Pew Research shows that one-third of Americans are currently concerned about the safety and stability of US financial institutions whereas 56% think banks and financial institutions have negative effects on the economic situation of the country. This is just a glimpse of the negativities surrounding CeFi.

The traditional financial system works on the basis of trust. When trust in the financial system is shaken as a result of bank failures risking depositors' money, asset bubble bursts, and inflation eating away purchasing power, there needs to be a technological solution to make the economy work better. DeFi does just that. DeFi gets rid of trusted authorities to enable peer-to-peer financial transactions.

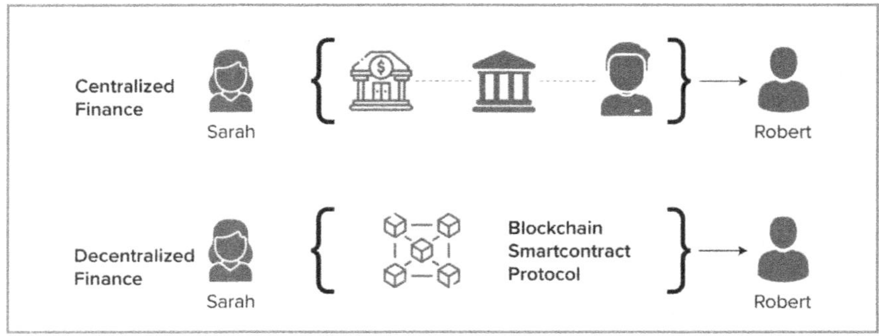

Figure 8: DeFi vs. CeFi (Source: Appinventiv)

Under CeFi, a bank takes deposits from savers and lends the money to borrowers, and earns from the interest rate differences. The borrowers are charged a higher interest than the rate paid to the depositors. Banks are also in complete control of depositors' money, which can lead to depositor's suffering the consequences of reckless investment decisions. In contrast, DeFi connects borrowers and savers, and lets them do transactions directly through smart contracts without the need for a bank. Both the borrower and the saver are better off as they save on transaction costs, have better control over their money (through private keys), and get a better deal (the borrowers can borrow at a lower interest and the savers can earn higher interest).

Moreover, DeFi allows more transparency as all transactions are on the public ledger and anybody can see it. On the contrary, the transactions of a financial institution or bank are shrouded under layers of secrecy with the stakeholders hardly having access to the larger picture. The recent bank failure in the US shows how a lack of transparency leads to reckless risk-taking and myopic investment decisions by them. The same happened during the 2007-08 global financial crisis when a lack of transparency led to excessive risk-taking.

Looks like DeFi's transparency can lead to a more stable financial system.

DeFi is open to all as anyone with an Internet connection can access dApps and avail themselves of financial services. On the contrary, you need to fill out detailed application forms with supporting documents to get access to traditional financial services. Also, you need to pass eligibility criteria like proof of residency. DeFi is open 24/7 and 365 days a year. CeFi services are accessible only a few hours a day. On the other hand, DeFi transactions are settled almost in real-time through smart contracts. CeFi has many manual processes which delay transaction settlements.

Another problem with CeFi that DeFi can solve is the lack of privacy in the former. Today, you cannot buy even a pair of socks from an e-commerce site without revealing a plethora of information - starting from your address, card details, identity, and a large volume of your online data being tracked by sophisticated web applications. With DeFi, you need to reveal a bare minimum amount of information and you can do transactions without a company like Amazon or Facebook collecting your personal details.

What can we do with DeFi?

Potentially, DeFi can be applied to every aspect of finance currently dominated by CeFi. DeFi can even reach the areas unserved by CeFi - for example, by providing loans to people without a credit history. Some of the most common current applications of DeFi are:

◇ Decentralized exchange (DEX)
◇ Sending and receiving payments across the globe
◇ Borrowing and lending funds
◇ Using stablecoins (cryptos pegged to real currencies like the dollar to stabilize their values)
◇ Saving and investing
◇ Earning additional income through staking or yield farming (locking crypto in a dApp to earn interest and other income)
◇ Trading and managing portfolios or cryptos, stocks, or other assets
◇ Buying and selling insurance
◇ Raising funds for business

The DeFi revolution picked up in 2020 and reached its pick by the end of 2021 when the total value locked (TVL) reached $256 billion. 2022 was a brutal year for cryptos. By the end of 2022, the total in DeFi was about $53 billion in more than 1,500 DeFi protocols. However, as the crypto market is steadily rebounding starting from 2023, we can expect more activities in the DeFi space.

Going by the latest numbers, decentralized exchanges (DEX) are the most widely used application of DeFi. The failure of centralized exchanges like FTX in 2022 has highlighted the potential dangers of centralized systems. In a DEX, like Uniswap which runs on Ethereum, users have complete control over their cryptos by having custody of their private keys. On November 14, 2023, 3 days after FTX filed for bankruptcy, Uniswap topped $1.1 billion in trading volume, surpassing Coinbase to become the second-largest crypto exchange. Beginning 2023, more than 34% of the total TVL in DeFi is related to DEXs. The next is the lending DeFis which constitutes around 20% of the total TVL.

DeFi and Ethereum

In April 2023, the prestigious business magazine Fortune launched 'Fortune Crypto 40', a first-of-its-kind benchmark for the crypto industry. The benchmark lists the top 5 crypto platforms in 8 categories. In the category called 'Protocol', Ethereum comes at the top spot followed by Bitcoin and Polygon Labs. In the DeFi category, the top platforms are - Uniswap Labs, Lido, MakerDAO, Aave, and Curve. What is common among all these 5 platforms is that they all run on the Ethereum blockchain!

If we have to write Ethereum's contribution to Defi in one sentence, it will read like this - Ethereum's smart contracts made DeFi possible, it pioneered DeFi, top DeFi protocols run on its blockchain, and it is the uncontested numero uno in DeFi applications. As of the end of 2022, Ethereum constitutes about 60% of Defi's TVL. Tron comes at a distance 2nd with only 9.8% of TVL.

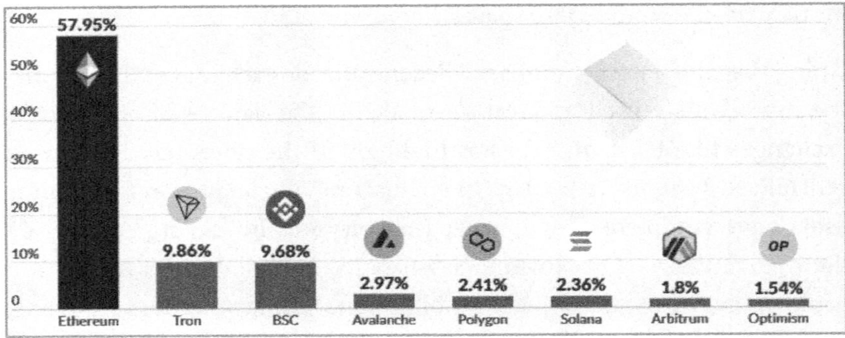

Figure 9: *Ethereum's DeFi •ominance (Source:banklesstimes.com)*

One of the central working mechanisms of DeFi is replacing trusted authorities with technology. However, this is only possible when contracts can be created, executed, and enforced without a third party. Ethereum's smart contracts do just that. Ethereum provides the technical backbone for DeFi to proliferate and solve inefficiencies associated with the traditional financial system. Ethereum, with its largest base of users and developers, has been successfully carrying forward its legacy in DeFi, and the associated dApps. With the planned upgrades like sharding and layer 2s, Ethereum will be able to process more transactions, and that too at a lower cost. This will strengthen Ethereum's competitive advantage in DeFi.

As of January 2023, there are about 6.7 million DeFi users in the world. The number may look minuscule compared to the number of users of traditional financial services. However, DeFi's projected annual growth of more than 45% can create a significantly large user base within a few years. Exponential growth can be achieved through network effect as more users jump in pushing the value of ETH higher. So, when next time crypto critics point out the failure of crypto platforms like FTX to denounce DeFi, we must show them JP Morgan's Crypto Report (November 2022) that states "*...while the news of the collapse of FTX is empowering crypto skeptics, we woul• point out that all of the recent collapses in the crypto ecosystem have been from centralize• players an• not from •ecentralize• protocols.*" DeFi is not the problem, it is the solution.

Let's now look at Non-Fungible Tokens (NFTs), a new-age digital asset made possible by Ethereum's smart contracts.

Chapter 09

NON-FUNGIBLE TOKENS (NFTS) - CREATING VALUE THROUGH SCARCITY AND OWNERSHIP

Nobody ever changed the world by doing
what everyone else was doing.
- ***Mark Cuban,*** *American Entrepreneur, and Investor.*

Figure 10: *The First 5,000 Days by Beeple (Source: The New York Times)*

Christie's, founded in 1766 by Scottish auctioneer James Christie, is the largest auction house in the world. It has sold 8 of the 10 most important single-owner art collections in history. In 2017, Christie's sold Leonardo da Vinci's Salvator Mundi for a record $450 million, making it the highest price paid for any artwork ever. 2 years later, the London-based auction house sold Jeff Koons's Rabbit, a 3 ft high sculpture made of stainless steel, for $91 million. It was the costliest sale of any artwork by a living artist. But in March 2021, something unique was auctioned at Christie's for the very first time in its 255 years of history. It wasn't any of da Vinci's masterpieces or Raphael's gems - rather, it is a digital collage by a graphic designer which was sold for a whopping $69 million, entirely paid with Ether (ETH).

May 01, 2007 - American digital artist Mike Winkelmann, commonly known by his pseudonym Beeple, started posting one piece of digital art daily. He continued doing so for the next 13 and a half years. Then in 2021, he created his digital magnum opus called 'The First 5,000 Days' by combining these 5,000 'Everyday' images and creating something alien - a Non-Fungible Token (NFT). The auction at Christie's, which saw 33 bidders (two-thirds of which were millennials), finally fetched $69,346,250. Going by this price, Mike Winkelmann is now among the top 3 living artists, along with Jeff Koons, and David Hockney.

NFT is the new-age digital asset for artists and all sorts of content creators on the Internet.

Figure 11: *Kitty by Paris Hilton (Source: cryptograph.com)*

Paris Hilton is no Pablo Picasso. Neither are cat pictures any rare on the Internet. A simple Google search on 'cat drawings' gives us 1,250,000,000 results! But, what if there is only one original piece of the above cat drawing, only one person can own it and the ownership is immutably established on the blockchain? This can make it relatively scarce, and the proud owner now has the bragging rights on this newly minted digital asset. This is the essence of an NFT. So, a not-so-professional digital drawing by the famous American media personality was sold for $17,000 as an Ethereum-based NFT. Someone out there felt the ownership right is worth the high price. Similarly, there are buyers in the market willing to pay $1,700 for American entrepreneur Mark Cuban's quote at the beginning of the chapter.

In the world of NFTs, an NBA special moment, like a short clip of LeBron James dunking, sells for $208 thousand, a pixelated CryptoPunk (a famous NFT collection of pixel art images) gets auctioned for $1.5 million, or buyers are willing to shell out as much as $2.9 million for a Tweet by Twitter's co-founder Jack Dorsey. Celebrities from Lindsay Lohan to Snoop Dogg and companies from Nike and Coca-Cola to

Gucci, Lamborghini, and Louis Vuitton are all part of this NFT craze. NFTs worth around $2 billion were traded in March 2023 alone. According to Morgan Stanley, NFTs are going to be a $240 billion market by 2030.

So, what is this hype about NFTs? Do they have any fundamental value or is it just another asset bubble? And what does Ethereum have to do with NFTs?

Let's find the answers.

First of all, what is an NFT?

The concept of an NFT is centered around digital scarcity, ownership, and authenticity. The value of an asset depends on how authentic and scarce it is. Look at the Internet. Billions of users are generating online content - writing blogs, creating social media posts, making Tik-Tok videos, developing cat GIFs, or sharing digital art of different forms. Most of this content is easily available for others to copy, download, edit, and use according to their individual needs.

We can easily download a cat picture from the Internet (without caring about who the actual owner is), put it as wallpaper on our phones, or edit it to make a meme. Since these digital commodities are seemingly endless in supply, we place very little value on them. When something can be easily copied, downloaded, and edited, it's very difficult to establish who owns what. But what if there is a mechanism to establish ownership of digital assets? This can create a relative scarcity. And whatever is scarce, is valuable. To reiterate the main point, what an NFT does is create value through digital scarcity by establishing authenticity and ownership.

In technical terms, NFTs help in tokenizing any asset (digital or physical) to establish its ownership with a digital identifier on a blockchain. Before delving more into the intricacies of NFTs, let's understand two related economic terms - fungible and non-fungible.

A fungible item is anything that's interchangeable with another item of similar nature. A $1 bill in your purse is of the same value as another $1 bill in anyone's purse. You can easily interchange one bill with the other of the same dollar value. Therefore, the dollar, like bitcoin (BTC) or ETH, is fungible.

But what about the famous portrait of the Mona Lisa hanging on the wall of the Louvre? It's one of a kind. Can it be interchanged with anything else? With any artwork of another artist or of da Vinci himself? Non-fungible items are unique items that cannot be interchanged for another. So even if there are millions of cat images on the Internet, there is only one by the name 'Kitty' drawn by the famous American businesswoman Paris Hilton. This is a non-fungible asset. Other examples of non-fungible assets are a sea-facing house in a specific location, a designer cloth, a music video, a piece of art, a poem written by Abraham Lincoln, or a selfie of Lindsay Lohan. NFTs come into the picture when we tokenize a non-fungible asset i.e., create a blockchain-based token representing the asset and establishing its ownership.

Figure 12: *Fungible vs. Non-fungible (Source: thehustle.co)*

So even though you can still download, copy or use Hilton's drawing (like we did for this book), the ownership of this piece of art remains with the owner of the NFT. Through NFTs, the blockchain records the important unique details of the item, identifies its current and past owners, and makes buying and selling seamless through cryptos. More interestingly, the smart contract in the NFTs can program a royalty mechanism through which the original creator (like Paris Hilton or Beeple) can keep receiving royalties with every resale.

NFTs include unique digital identifiers that act as proof of ownership for an asset. NFTs are permanently recorded in a blockchain, and they cannot be modified, duplicated, or substituted. Owners can tokenize assets like digital art, drawings, written content, music, videos, reels, or even real estate in the metaverse (coming to this shortly). It's a permanent digital certificate of ownership and authenticity of an asset, which can be digital or even physical.

The history of NFTs goes back to the Colored Coin project on the Bitcoin network in 2012, of which Vitalik Buterin was a member. It was an effort to establish asset ownership using Bitcoin's blockchain. However, Bitcoin's limited programmability was a big hindrance. NFTs came into the limelight starting in 2017 when Larva Labs studio came up with an NFT collection called CryptoPunks. The 2020-21 crypto bull run led to tremendous growth in NFTs along with other crypto projects. According to DappRadar, NFT sales took a giant leap from a meager $94.9 million in 2020 to $25.1 billion in 2021. Even though the entire crypto market went through a severe bear market in 2022, total NFT sales were $24.7 billion, almost the same as in 2021. Going by the number of trades, 101 million NFT trades took place in 2022 compared to 58.6 million in 2021 - about a 70% rise when the overall crypto market was down by a similar percentage.

How do NFTs work?

NFTs represent ownership of unique items and are permanently recorded on a blockchain, most commonly Ethereum. So, how is ownership of an NFT established?

Suppose you made a short video of your cat dancing in the rain with a rainbow in the background and you think it can be a valuable asset. You can create an NFT to establish that you are the rightful owner of this unique content. The process of creating an NFT is called 'minting' in which your asset (here, it's your cat video) is represented on the blockchain. Smart contracts are the primary means through which developers mint NFTs. The majority of NFTs are minted on the Ethereum blockchain.

If you want to mint an NFT, you first need to have a crypto wallet (like Metamask) because you have to spend a certain amount of cryptos as transaction fees. Your NFTs will be stored in your wallet, which is protected by a private key. Next, you need to select an NFT marketplace like OpenSea (the largest NFT marketplace by the number of users) which allows trading of the NFTs. Now, you need to upload your file on the NFT marketplace and your NFT will be created. Then you can put a selling price for your NFTs. Smart contracts manage an NFT's ownership and transferability. Metadata contained in NFTs mention the unique features of the item and its unique ID, and map it to a unique owner ID. The blockchain records who owns an NFT currently, its previous owners, its attributes, and its transferability.

What are NFT's value propositions?

In February 2022, South Korea's Hoseo University announced that the graduate batch of 2021 wouldn't receive a paper-based diploma/ transcript of records. Rather, the academic credentials of all the 2,830 graduates would be minted as NFTs and transferred to their respective crypto wallets. The 45-year old university believes a shift to blockchain-based degrees would make it easier for students to access administrative services, get the degrees verified by prospective employers and prevent alteration or forgery. A paper-based diploma/transcript of records can be easily duplicated but an NFT minted by a university stating a student's credentials are permanently recorded on the blockchain and verifiable by the members of the public. Since then, a number of other educational institutions like Israel's College of Management Academic Studies and Ireland's Trinity Business School have followed suit.

Turns out that NFTs have much wider and more serious applications beyond cat and ape pictures. The world's largest education company Pearson is turning its titles into NFTs to profit from second-hand sales while consulting major Ernst & Young is promoting fine wine investing by establishing the wine's authenticity through NFTs.

How do NFTs create value?

NFTs create value primarily through their 3 main features - they are verifiable through cryptography, are unique and scarce, and are easy to transfer. When ownership of assets can be ascertained and recorded in a public ledger, it would create scarcity for an asset, which in turn would drive its value. For thousands of years, people have been collecting antiques, rare coins, artworks like paintings, and even precious stones. In more recent years, we see people collecting antique cars, vintage guitars, autographed baseballs, stamps, sneakers, and even older models of iPhones.

The traditional method of establishing ownership of these collectibles has been a piece of paper issued by a centralized authority. Such papers can be lost, stolen, or forged. Also, the transfer of ownership can be a big hassle. NFTs solve all these problems. Artists can create unique digital assets, establish ownership and trade with others. This creates a liquid market for digital collectibles and a new asset class.

One astounding feature of NFTs is that the smart contract can include royalty terms. So any subsequent sale of an NFT can generate a royalty for the original creator. This is a great deal for artists and content creators. In addition to trading and earning royalties, NFTs, similar to cryptos, can be staked to earn interest income. NFTs open additional avenues of income at a time when most people are trying to diversify income sources and have multiple passive sources of income.

The value of NFTs is going to be even more pronounced with rapid growth in Web3 and the Metaverse. Web 1.0 (1990-2004) was read-only. This meant users didn't have many contributions. It was a one-way flow of information. Then came Web 2.0 (2004 - now) which saw a rise in user-generated content with social media and other user platforms like Facebook, YouTube, and TikTok. Anybody can create and share content on Web 2.0 - however, the ownership right isn't established, and large platforms are mainly in control of this content. Web 3.0 changes that. This new avatar of the Internet is gradually emerging as we not only want to create and share content, but we want to own and trade it with others. Establishing ownership rights is crucial for Web3. And when it comes to establishing digital ownership in a permanent way, NFT is our best hope so far.

The Metaverse is a 3D virtual world, aided by technologies like augmented reality (AR) and virtual reality (VR), in which billions of people would be able to collaborate, shop, connect to each other, work, play games, and many more through their virtual avatars. On the metaverse, you can buy your virtual real estate, build a virtual world, and even conduct a music concert. It's arguably the future of the Internet, entertainment, and social media. NFTs would establish ownership of your digital assets (such as virtual real estate, in-game collectibles, virtual characters, and virtual content) on the metaverse. According to DappRadar, the value of the real estate in the metaverse appreciated by 500% in 2021 - the same year social media giant Facebook committed $10 billion to its metaverse project. The intense focus on the virtual world is one of the reasons the company changed its name to Meta. Moreover, companies like Google, Microsoft, Nvidia, and Qualcomm are heavily invested in their respective metaverse projects. Consulting major McKinsey expects the metaverse economy to reach $5 trillion by 2030. NFTs can be an essential growth engine for the metaverse by authenticating digital assets and making trade possible.

Moreover, NFTs are being increasingly integrated with industries like digital arts, collectibles, gaming, luxury fashion, virtual worlds, events, sports, social media, and even logistics. For example, NFTs make it possible for you to own in-game collectibles and monetize your progress in a game on a dApp. Similarly, the fashion industry is tokenizing its new collections in the metaverse. According to Morgan Stanley, luxury NFTs are going to be worth $25 billion by 2030.

As mentioned before, in addition to digital assets NFTs can also be used to tokenize real-world assets like precious metals, commodities, currencies, land, and art collection. Today, someone looking to add gold to their investment portfolio can do so by buying physical gold or investing in Gold ETFs or derivatives. Securing and trading physical gold has security concerns as well as many hassles. Also, trading gold ETFs and derivates have drawbacks like liquidity and costs. However, the tokenization of gold resolves these issues and provides many added advantages. According to Alkesh Shah and Andrew Moss, analysts at the Bank of America, *tokenized gold provides exposure to physical gold, 24/7 real-time settlement, no management fees, and no storage or insurance costs. The low minimum investment increases accessibility and fractionalization enables the transfer of physical gold ownership and value that was not previously possible.* According to a report by Bank of America, the tokenized gold market surpassed a $1 billion valuation in March 2023.

Real estate is another asset class that can immensely benefit from tokenization through NFTs. It's a capital-intensive illiquid asset with a number of transaction barriers. There are issues like legal hurdles, lack of transparency, and transaction delays. The problems are even more serious in developing countries where land records may not be adequate. Tokenization can establish ownership and make transactions transparent. It can also lower counter-party risk and increase liquidity.

Most importantly, tokenization makes it possible to fragment ownership of a large property into smaller units via the blockchain. For example, $1 million worth of land can be represented through 1000 tokens worth $1,000 each. Each token would represent a fraction of the entire property. We can fragment ownership of large pieces of expensive commercial properties like shopping malls and multi-story apartments through NFTs. This will make the real estate market more liquid by attracting retail investors.

Ethereum's NFT dominance

Smart contracts are essential to the development of NFTs and Ethereum is the most established player in smart contracts. While blockchain platforms like Solana (SOL) and Cardano (ADA) support NFTs, Ethereum remains the number one choice for developers. In addition to smart contracts, the other reasons behind Ethereum's NFT dominance are its large developer community and well-established token standards. Ethereum Request for Comments (ERC) 721 is the main token standard behind NFTs. ERCs document technical standards and guidelines for Ethereum developers.

According to data from BanklessTimes, a blockchain news portal, Ethereum accounted for 78 percent of the total NFT sales volume in December 2022. In the words of Jonathan Merry, CEO of CryptoMonday, *Ethereum's share of the market in•icates that investors are confi•ent in the platform's ability to grow an• scale. It also has a first-mover a•vantage, which can be •ifficult for other projects to overcome.* Going by DappRadar's report on blockchain and decentralized application (dApp) adoption, in 2022 more than 21.2 million NFT transactions took place in the Ethereum ecosystem. OpenSea and Blur, two of the leading NFT marketplaces, are primarily based on Ethereum.

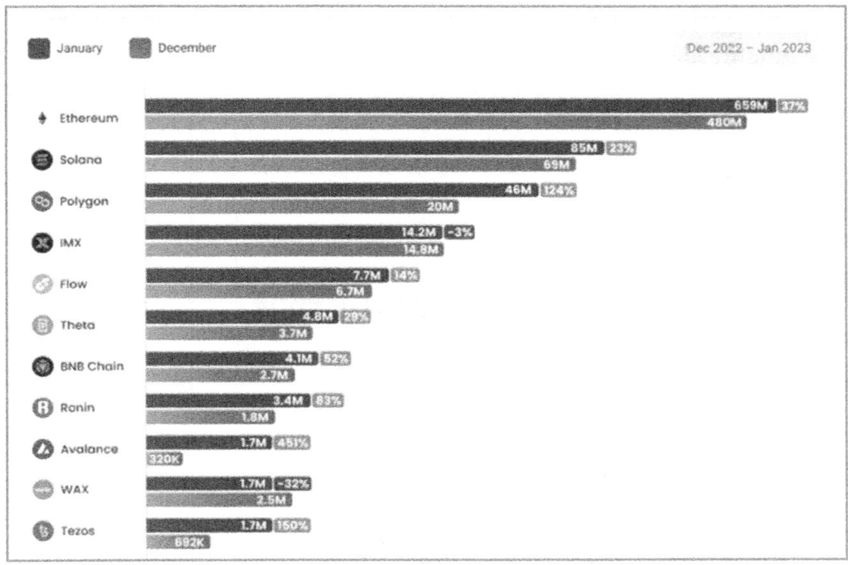

Figure 13: *Top NFT blockchains by trading volume in January 2023 (Source: DappRadar)*

As we mentioned before, you need a certain amount of ETH to mint NFTs on the Ethereum ecosystem. Hence one of the indicators of Ethereum's NFT dominance is the portion of NFT transactions compared to all transactions on Ethereum. According to CryptoSlate, an NFT data aggregator, in January 2023, 28% of gas usage (transaction fees paid) on Ethereum was related to NFTs while DeFi (with 8% of total gas usage) came second. This means more than one-fourth of transaction fees received by Ethereum came from NFT-based transactions.

NFT is a demand-side factor for ETH. Growth in NFTs will not only expand the Ethereum ecosystem but increase the demand for ETH, pushing its price higher. The fact that total NFT transactions increased by about 70% in 2022 despite a grueling crypto bear market is a huge bullish factor for Ethereum. However, with a rise in crypto domains like NFTs and DeFi, there is going to be increasing pressure on the Ethereum ecosystem to process transactions faster and at a lower cost. This means there is a need for greater scalability.

Let's see how Ethereum is augmenting scalability through Layer 2 implementation.

Chapter 10

ADDRESSING SCALABILITY THROUGH LAYER-2 (L2) SOLUTIONS

Scalability isn't important until it suddenly is.
Decentralization isn't important until it suddenly is.
Privacy isn't important until it suddenly is.
*- **Naval Ravikant,** Indian-American entrepreneur and investor.*

American author John Gall was not an expert on technologies, let alone blockchain or distributed ledger. In fact, for most of his professional life, he was a practicing pediatrician with a special interest in parenting strategies. In an active career spanning over four decades, Gall wrote several papers and books on child development and parenting. But besides pediatrics, he also had a curious interest in the intricacies of system design. Gall made an interesting observation on how complex systems work, which eventually became famous as Gall's law. The law states:

> *A complex system that works is invariably found to have evolved from a simple system that works. The inverse proposition also appears to be true: A complex system designed from scratch never works and cannot be made to work.*

Even though Gall's law is not meant for any specific domain, we can apply it to understand developments in blockchain technologies, especially Ethereum. The 'world computer' started with a simpler design and then evolved to assume a more complex structure - improving continuously as newer demands arose.

When blockchain platforms like Bitcoin and Ethereum started, scalability was not much of a concern. The initial focus was mainly on decentralization and privacy. But with a rapid increase in adoption, the natural question was - would these platforms be able to serve the needs of 8 billion human beings? For any blockchain platform to solve real-world problems, it must support a large volume of transactions. Visa, the gold standard in transaction processing, currently handles an average of 150 million daily transactions. It can process up to 24,000 transactions in a second. In comparison, Ethereum processes around 1.1 million transactions a day. Its current number of transactions per second (TPS) is up to 30. Bitcoin, with a TPS of 7, is much slower.

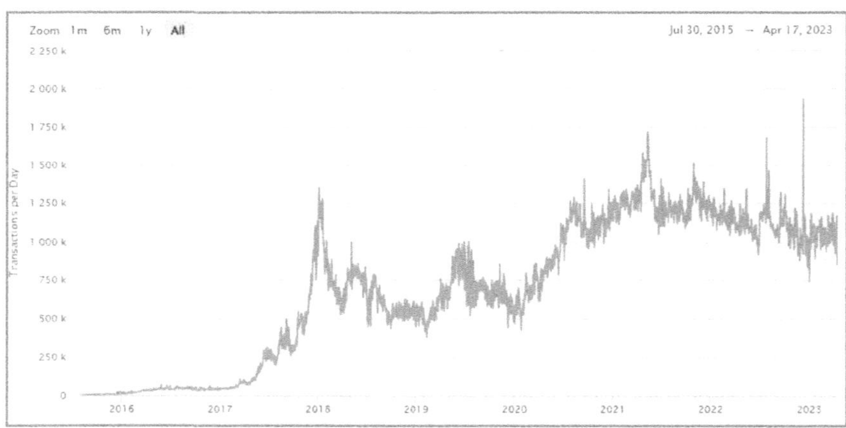

Figure 14: *Ethereum daily transactions: 2015-2023 (Source: Ethereum.org)*

Scalability is not a big challenge in a centralized system like Visa. The platform has complete control over the processing of its transactions. A blockchain like Ethereum is different. Being a distributed database with timestamps of transactions, each node in the network needs to keep a copy of the entire ledger to ensure decentralization and security.

So, the main advantages of a blockchain (decentralization and security) actually act as a disadvantage when it comes to scalability. This is why we have the blockchain trilemma that we discussed earlier in the book.

The problem of scalability was not an acute one in the beginning, when the structure of Ethereum was relatively simple. As more developers and users came onboard, the problems of scalability and high transaction costs became more significant. Thus, there was a need to add more layers to an initially simple design to create a more complex system that worked better. This is why there needed to be an iterative approach in which different problems are solved in different stages.

Ethereum's philosophy has been to improve incrementally. Ethereum has built on its simple structure to create a more sophisticated one that addresses various challenges through multiple upgrades and integration of new technologies. Upgrades like the London fork, Beacon chain, or the Merge addressed the scalability problem in stages. Now, since the utmost focus of the platform is on transaction speed and gas fees, different scalability solutions are being explored. This has led to Layer 2 (L2) solutions becoming the most promising way to address scalability for Ethereum.

So, what is L2 scaling and how does it work? Let's look for the answers.

Off-chain vs. on-chain scaling solutions

In blockchains, similar to any transaction-processing system, scaling means increasing transaction speed as well as the TPS. Simply said, scaling enables the platform to process more transactions in a given time and each transaction takes lower system time. There are 2 broad ways to achieve these - one is internal and the other one is external.

Think of a busy highway on which traffic congestion is a recurring problem. But we want more vehicles to pass through it every hour. Solutions could include improving the existing road by repairing damages like potholes, broadening the road, or allowing only smaller vehicles. But what if there are no further ways of improving the highway or making it any wider? We need to think of alternatives like creating an alternate bypass road to divert a part of the traffic. Similarly, in blockchains, some of the scaling solutions involve improving the existing blockchain to make it more scalable, while others involve deploying techniques outside the blockchain. The first set of scaling solutions is called on-chain scaling while the other set is called off-chain scaling.

In on-chain scaling, we try to make the blockchain more efficient through a number of techniques. For example, we can increase the block sizes to contain more transactions in a block. We can even shrink the amount of data generated by each transaction. Both approaches can improve scalability. Sharding is another promising technique in which the entire blockchain is divided into smaller sub-parts and each sub-part processes a fraction of the transactions. This way, sharding helps in the parallel processing of tasks, resulting in higher throughput and transaction speed. But on-chain scaling solutions come with certain drawbacks like less decentralization and increased security issues. When all transactions don't need to be validated by all nodes, decentralization is compromised. Moreover, it's easier to attack a smaller segment than the entire network. Consequently, sharding increases the probability of a single point of failure. Additionally, we cannot keep increasing block sizes or shrinking transaction data indefinitely.

We need to look for additional scaling solutions elsewhere.

Off-chain scaling solutions are applied outside the main blockchain. Precisely, these scaling solutions focus on keeping the decentralization and security level intact while getting more transactions processed externally. An advantage of off-chain scaling is that we don't need to make any changes to the blockchain while making it more scalable. Layer 2s are an off-chain scaling solution, which offers the highest scaling potential for Ethereum at this point.

Let's dig deeper into Layer 2 blockchains.

Layer-2 (L2) scaling solutions

In October 2021, during the Shanghai International Blockchain Week, Ethereum's founder Vitalik Buterin acknowledged the need for an immediate scaling-up of Ethereum. However, he said, on-chain solutions like sharding can take a long time. So, in the near term, his focus was on L2 solutions. The vision seems to be quite right as it has been showing promising results.

A blockchain platform like Ethereum is an ecosystem with many components working and interacting simultaneously. Figure 15 illustrates the functioning of a blockchain ecosystem with respect to multiple layers. Layer 0 (L0) consists of networking tools that make blockchain possible in the first place. L0 is built on the hardware layer. Layer 1 (L1) is the base blockchain (also called mainnet or base layer) in which transactions are verified and recorded using a consensus mechanism. Blockchains like Ethereum and Bitcoin are L1 blockchains as they focus on two central aspects of blockchain - decentralization, and security.

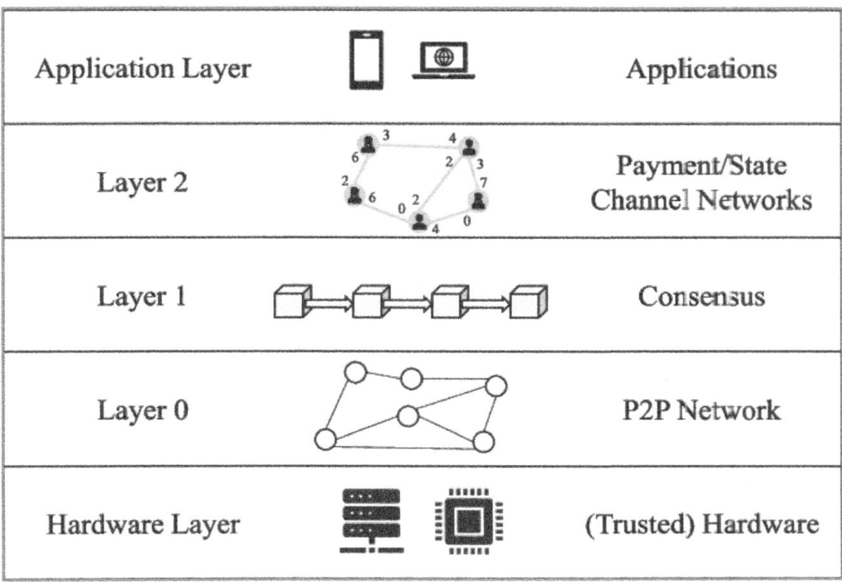

Figure 15: *Layered architecture of a blockchain ecosystem (Source: Researchgate)*

However, because of the blockchain trilemma we discussed earlier, the L1 blockchains are easily clogged when transaction volume goes up. In a centralized payment processing like Visa, transaction costs generally remain fixed; however, Ethereum has a dynamic transaction cost. So, when more transactions queue up in the system, the gas price goes up - forcing users to pay more for using Ethereum. This is the reason that in recent years high gas prices and lack of scalability have been two main concerns for the ecosystem. But what if we can add another layer on top of L1 and share a part of the transaction load on this layer?

This is exactly what L2 does.

L2 blockchains are built on top of L1 to make transactions faster and cheaper. Simply said, L2 is an additional blockchain that is built on L1 to share its workload. It extends the existing blockchain. The rollups on Ethereum (coming to this shortly) and Bitcoin lightning networks (a second layer on Bitcoin to process payments faster) are examples of L2 solutions. It turns out that while L1 blockchains are great at ensuring security and decentralization, they are easily clogged due to very high transaction burdens. For example, Ethereum's gas price spiked wildly during the 2020-21 crypto bull market when transaction volume reached a record high.

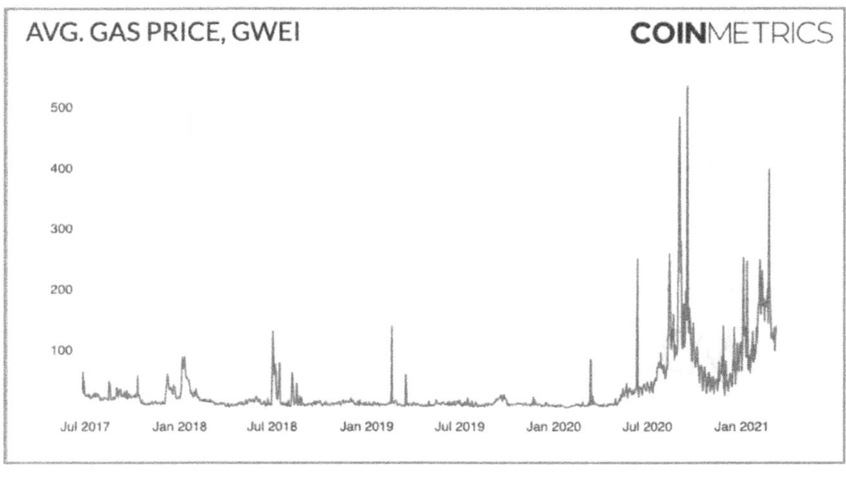

Figure 16: *Spike in Ethereum gas price (Source: coinmetrics.io)*

When we combine L1 and L2, we can resolve the blockchain trilemma. L2s don't compete with L1s. Rather they complement each other. According to Dmitry Shklovsky, co-founder of the blockchain development platform QuickNode, *L1s typically prioritize security and decentralization over scalability. L2s reduce the workload on the main chain, making the network faster and more user-friendly, allowing chains to scale quickly without compromising decentralization or security.*

L2 blockchains are basically third-party protocols that are lighter and not burdened with the complexities of L1. For example, in February 2023, the world's second largest crypto exchange, Coinbase, launched its Ethereum-based L2 blockchain called Base. It's a 'secure, low-cost, and developer-friendly blockchain' that allows developers to build various dApps on Ethereum. Deployment of L2s on Ethereum's mainnet can increase activities (more DeFis, dApps, and NFTs) on Ethereum by making it faster and cost-effective. L2s make Ethereum more accessible for developers and end-users.

How do L2s work?

L2 blockchains are built at the top of L1 blockchains to remove constraints and lower bottlenecks. But processing transactions faster is not the only goal of Ethereum - there needs to be decentralization and security. L2s cannot provide decentralization and privacy as they are not equipped with these techniques. They don't record transactions on the blockchain. L2s process transactions and then report them to the L1 to permanently record them on the mainnet. So there needs to be seamless communication between L1 and L2s.

An L2 regularly communicates with L1 by sending bundles of transactions to be recorded on the mainnet. L2s handle the transaction burden and then send the final proof back to the Ethereum mainnet. This ensures that security and decentralization of the overall ecosystem are maintained while we achieve greater scalability. Let's take a simple analogy to understand this. When you are overburdened with work at the office, you can hire subordinates to share some of the workload.

The subordinates are required to report back to you daily or weekly on the status of the ongoing tasks. This ensures that more tasks are completed on time while you keep an eye on them through a reporting system. Similarly, L2 takes on the transaction burden thereby making the entire ecosystem faster and cheaper, while L1 controls security and decentralization.

In July 2022, Polygon introduced its L2 solution zkEVM which is expected to lower Ethereum's gas fees by as much as 90%. zkEVM stands for Zero-Knowledge Ethereum Virtual Machine. Zero-knowledge is a rollup technique for reporting data from L2 to L1. Ethereum Virtual Machine (EVM) is the computer system that runs Ethereum's smart contracts. The Polygon zkEVM batches large number of transactions into a single bulk transaction before relaying the same to Ethereum L1 for recording. The gas fee of this single bulk transaction is shared among all the individual transactions in the batch. So more transactions are processed at a given time while transaction cost is also trimmed drastically. Anything that can be done on the Ethereum mainnet can also be done on the L2 - but most importantly, done faster and cheaper.

Optimistic rollups and zero-knowledge (ZK) rollups

While processing transactions, L2s do not send every transaction on the L1 at the time of processing. Rather, L2s roll up transactions into bundles and send them for recording to the L1 chain at regular intervals. There are different rollup techniques - the methods through which transactions are reported to L1. Two of the most common techniques are optimistic rollups and zero-knowledge (ZK) rollups.

Optimistic rollups, as the name says, are based on the optimism that all data is correct. It deploys a waiting period in which transactions can be reversed. All the data is added to the ledger after the waiting period. ZK rollups generate cryptographic receipts to confirm transactions are authentic without leaking the specifics. This is why this technique is called 'zero knowledge'. ZK rollups are more secure but technologically complex compared to optimistic rollups. Currently, most L2 solutions on Ethereum are based on optimistic rollups because of their simplicity. However, moving forward there would be more ZK rollups because of their superior security features.

Ethereum's L2 solutions in action

Scalability and decreasing transaction costs have been Ethereum's main priorities for the last several years. Crypto's no. 2 plans to expand scalability through L2 solutions. Currently, several L2 blockchains like Arbitrum, Optimism, Boba Network, Loopring, zkSync, ZKSpace, and Aztec are deployed on top of Ethereum. Out of these, Arbitrum and Optimism are the largest ones in terms of the total number of transactions and the total value locked (TVL).

As of April 20, 2023, the total value locked (TVL) in all Ethereum L2 solutions is $9.74 billion, which is about one-third of Ethereum's DeFi TVL. The leading duo Arbitrum and Optimism make up around 90% of the TVL in Ethereum L2s. The growth in Ethereum L2 solutions is so rapid that the L2 TVL increased by about 40% in the last 30 days (as of April 20,2023).

Recently, activities on the Ethereum L2s have surpassed the transaction volume on the base layer. On April 20, 2023, the mainnet processed 1.07 million transactions compared to more than 2.6 million transactions processed by L2s. Out of these, Arbitrum (1.8 million) and Optimism (about 0.3 million) carried out more than 2.1 million transactions.

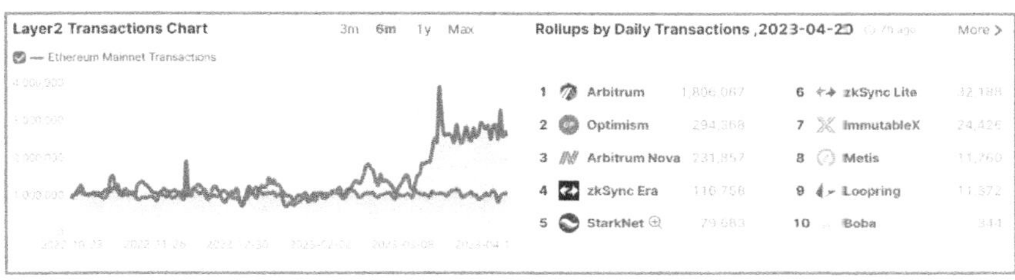

Figure 17: Ethereum L1 vs. L2 transactions (Source: orbiter.finance)

L2s have consistently increased Ethereum's TPS. As of April 2023, the scaling factor is around 4. This means L2s have increased Ethereum's throughput (TPS) by a factor of 4. Potentially, L2s can increase Ethereum's TPS by a factor of hundreds or even thousands. Moreover, as Figure 18 shows, the L2 scaling solutions have helped stabilize Ethereum's transaction fees in recent months to a great extent.

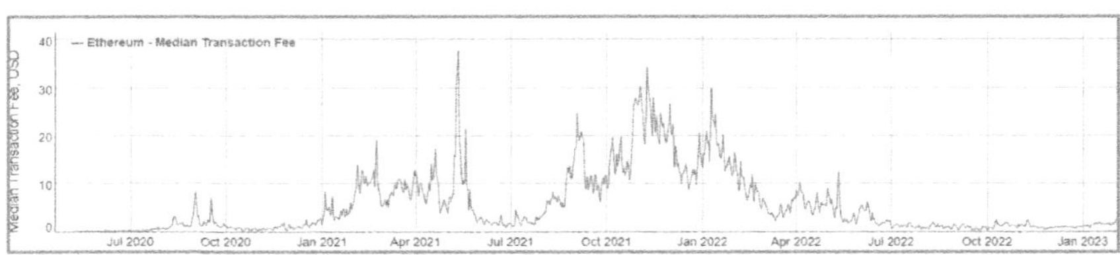

Figure 18: *Ethereum's me•ian transaction cost (Source: bitinfocharts.com)*

An important point we have reiterated multiple times in the book is that scalability is essential for Ethereum's future growth and value creation. L2s, along with other on-chain and off-chain scaling solutions, have been showing awesome results in improving Ethereum's scalability. The future roadmap of the Ethereum foundation has a clear focus on building on these improvements to make Ethereum much more scalable. Following Gall's law, it's on track to adding more on top solutions to build a more expandable, secure, economical, and decentralized crypto economy. In the words of Nick Bishop, director of NotCentralised, a web3 venture studio - *No chain has surpasse• Ethereum in ecosystem brea•th an• flexibility of smart contract •eployment. Ethereum will sink further •own in the web3 tech stack to a foun•ational, secure set of rails on top of which L2, L3, an• L4 iterations will flourish.*

Chapter 11

NAVIGATING THROUGH TREACHEROUS WATERS - AVOIDING CRYPTO SCAMS

Rather fail with honor than succeed by fraud.
- ***Sophocles.***

When CEOs communicate directly with investors and customers, the message sounds more genuine It creates impact and builds trust. So when crypto trading company Maxpread Technologies started its operations, it posted a video message by its CEO on YouTube. Michael Vanes, the middle-aged leader of the crypto platform, has a bald head and sports a nicely trimmed salt-and-pepper beard. The video shows him speaking in a soft monotone for about seven minutes. With an emotionless stare, he announced - *communicating with the most influential entrepreneurs around the world, we managed to make sure once again that the current moment is the best for the official launch of Maxpread Technologies.* Perfect script and perfect delivery - until, the California Department of Financial Protection and Innovation (DFPI) smelled something fishy.

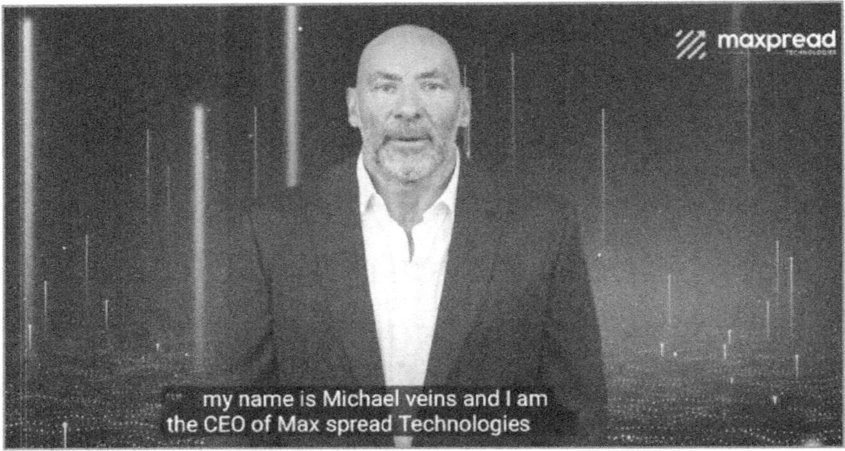

Figure 19: *AI-Generate• CEO of Maxprea• (Source: •ecrypt.co)*

An investigation by the department found that Michael Vanes was not the CEO of the company. In fact, the confident speaker in the video touting the profitability of the company was not a real person - it was AI-generated! The DFPI, in its five-page cease-and-desist order, said, *In reality, this was a hoax. The in•ivi•ual in the vi•eo was not the company's CEO, but rather a fictitious, computer-generate• avatar programme• to recite a script.*

A 55-year-old Italian man living in Hong Kong hoped to meet the love of his life on Tinder. The financial consultant matched with an 'investment banker' from Singapore on the popular dating app. Daily conversations turned into an online romance that went on for a couple of weeks. They even exchanged their numbers and started contacting each other over WhatsApp. Then came the twist. The impersonator on the other side persuaded the man to sign up on a bogus crypto site. She promised the investment would 'provide high returns'. In February 2023, he transferred HK$14.2 million (US$1.8 million) to 9 different accounts controlled by her. But the promised high return never came. Eventually, it became clear that 'she' was not the romantic soulmate he was looking for. Rather, it was a scammer impersonating an attractive woman to dupe him.

46-year-old Brian Bruce did not know much about cryptocurrency - until, an 'investment expert' connected with him over the professional network LinkedIn. The man claimed to be working for a Fortune 500 company. In Bruce's words - *He looked very legitimate, started talking business with me, and knew the company I work at. He had a friend who went to the same university as me years ago, and so we really connected that way.* So after two weeks of conversations, the impersonator introduced Bruce to a crypto trading platform called Zebpayex.vip. They even created fake financial charts to convince Bruce that the investment was earning a stellar return. Over two weeks, Bruce, who works as a logistics manager, invested about $200,000. However, when he wanted to withdraw the profits, he was asked to pay more. It did not take Bruce much time to realize had been conned.

Financial scams are as old as finance itself. With time, they only get more sophisticated. While cryptos present you with a technology-driven trillion-dollar asset class, there are also potential grave dangers. According to the FBI's Internet Crime Report 2022, losses from crypto scams went up from $907 million in 2021 to $2.57 billion in 2022. The report says - *Crypto-investment scams saw unprecedented increases in the number of victims and dollar losses to these investors. Many victims have assumed massive debt to cover losses from these fraudulent investments and the most targeted age group reporting this type of scam are victims ages 30 to 49.* Of all the different types of financial scams reported in 2022, crypto scams had the highest growth rate of 183%. According to another report by Crypto Presales, a crypto data collector, investors have lost more than $8.9 billion since the inception of cryptos through various crypto scams. More than 70% of this total loss was incurred in 2021 and 2022. 3 of the 10 largest crypto hacks happened in 2022 alone. In one such heist in March 2022, cryptos worth $620 million were stolen by hackers from the crypto platform Ronin Network.

As crypto-related scams are on the constant rise, you must do your best to protect your hard-earned money. Let's first look at the common ways scammers can target you.

12 Common crypto scams

The first step towards being in the safe zone is to know the different ways and means through which scammers are likely to deceive you. Some crypto scams involve luring you to invest in crypto platforms controlled by scammers and then siphoning off the funds. Others involve getting access to your private keys to drain cryptos out of your wallets. Let's look at some of these scamming methods:

1. Bogus crypto projects

One of the most common ways of falling prey to crypto scams is being lured to invest in a fake crypto project. In the world of cryptos, it's not always easy to separate the wheat from the chaff. Scammers do their homework well to sound genuine. They can take multiple routes, most popularly social media, to target potential victims. Almost always, they would present a new crypto platform or project which can give you astounding returns in a short period. In many cases, these projects are even listed on genuine crypto exchanges to deceive unsuspecting investors. For example, a 2021 study showed that around 50% of tokens listed on Uniswap, the largest decentralized exchange, were fake.

In addition, scammers can build fake websites, copy whitepapers of genuine cryptos, or even use edited photos/videos of influential people, most popularly Elon Musk, to establish authenticity. They are also likely to brag about their earnings, lavish lifestyle, and the swanky sports cars from the 'high returns' they earned from the project. It's also common for them to show fake charts and graphs showing your investment is growing rapidly. Once you are convinced and you go all out to make a huge investment, the next thing that happens is you are barred from withdrawing your money and you are cut off from all communication channels.

2. The rug pull

In this scam, developers create a new crypto project that can potentially 'change the world', create hype on social media, get some influencers on board, and beat the drums in every way possible to create enough buzz in the market. Once many gullible investors, most likely first timers, come on board, the developers abruptly ditch the projects and exit with investors' funds. Investors are left with nothing but some worthless tokens. Rug pulls have similarities with bogus crypto scams and are very common in the NFT space. Once there are enough investors for a new NFT that has no fundamental value, the developers exit with all the money.

In 2022, developers of Frosties NFTs promised to stake tokens for investors, which would allow them to receive a part of the income, access to the metaverse, and many other benefits. Based on the promise, the project team sold 8,888 'icecream NFTs'. But after the sale was complete, investors found that all social media handles, Discord channels, and project websites were closed while the dubious team completely disappeared. Investors lost $1.4 million in this rug pull.

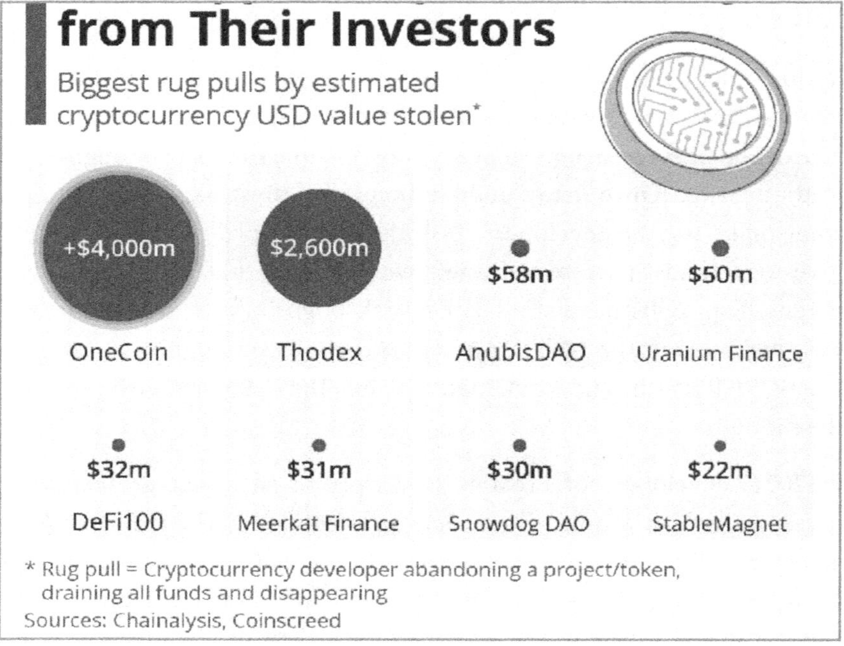

Figure 20: *Biggest crypto rug pulls. (Source: Chainalysis, Coinscree•)*

3. Pump-and-dump

It's an old price manipulation technique in investing which has found its place in cryptos too. The idea is to create a token and then artificially push its price higher to lure the crowd. The people behind these schemes gang up together with some big investors who buy the coin amongst themselves to manipulate its price and trading volume. When the price surges rapidly, the crypto gets more attention and many new investors jump in pushing the price even higher.

Once the token price is sky-high, the developers sell at the peak price and exit. What happens next is that the token price starts crashing and eventually they become almost worthless as there are no takers. An example of pump and dump is E-Coin. On February 6, 2018, the little-known cryptocurrency went up from $6 to $280 within a couple of hours before crashing back to $3 the next day. Figure 21 shows what a typical pump-and-dump scheme looks like.

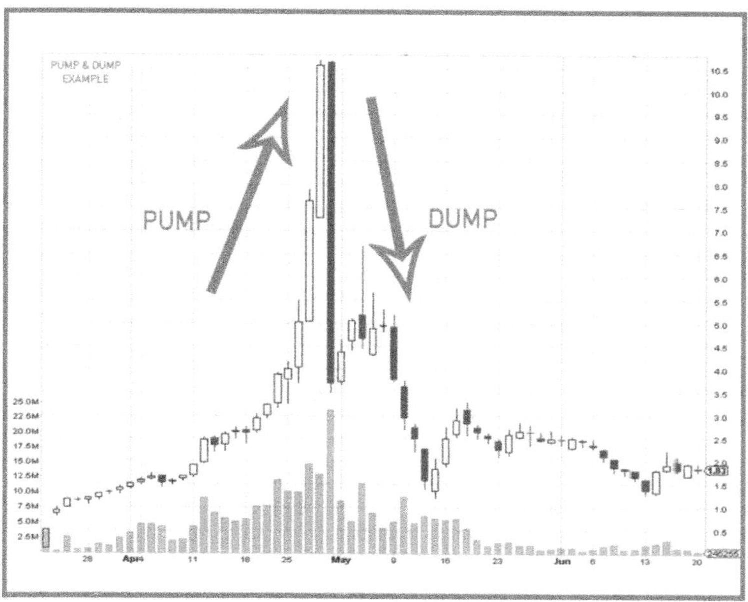

A typical graph for a coin that has been pumped & dumped

Figure 21: *Price movement due to pump and dump (Source: ICOholder)*

4. Dating scams

More people are using dating apps than ever. Nearly 370 million people used online dating services in 2022, a number estimated to reach 440 million by 2027. The leading dating app, Tinder, has about 75 million active monthly users. While online dating is easy and convenient, it's the new minefield of crypto scams.

In a typical dating scam, a scammer impersonates an attractive match and then builds a romantic relationship. After days or even weeks, the conversation is shifted to a more convenient medium like WhatsApp. Next, the impersonator introduces the target to a new crypto project, currency, token, or any other crypto asset which has recently earned them 'high returns'. Then the target is emotionally manipulated to invest in the project. In the beginning, the target is shown profits and how the investment is growing as promised. Eventually, once a large sum is invested - the impersonator blocks the target and cuts off all contact. Along with an eventual heartbreak, the target ends up with a huge financial dent.

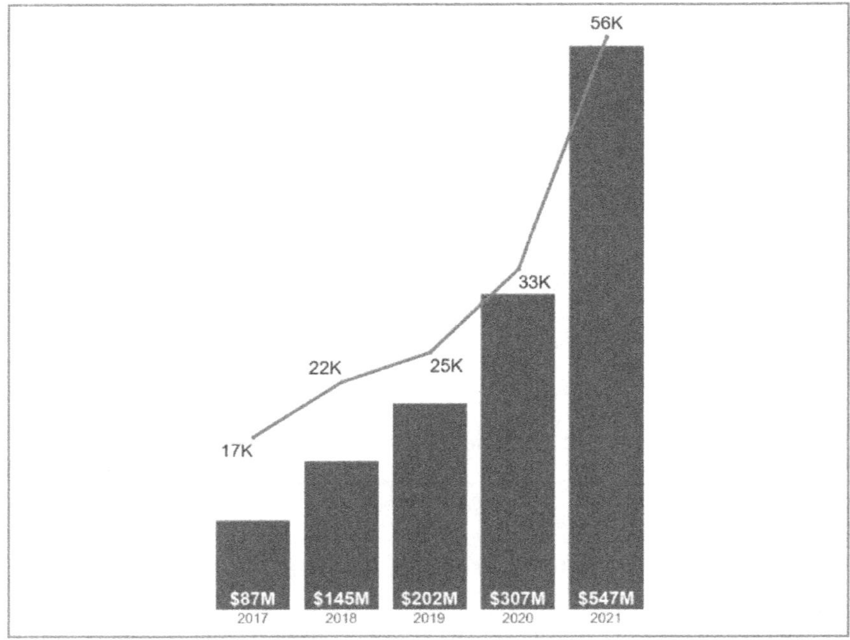

Figure 22: *Rising instances of romance scams (Source: Fe•eral Tra•e Commission)*

Currently, the romance scam is one of the highest reported crypto scams. A staggering $1.3 billion has been lost in various romance scams between 2017-21. In 2022, the FBI's Internet Crime Complaint Center (IC3), received complaints from a total of 19,050 victims reporting losses of over $739 million due to this scam. According to Sherri E. Onks, Special Agent in Charge of FBI Jacksonville, *online •ating is common to•ay, but unfortunately, scammers also thrive on those same sites.* She added - *whether you're looking for love or a frien•ship online, be sure you first un•erstan• the risk of being exploite•. Remember, a scammer will always eventually ask you for something, so set a boun•ary early on an• never, ever sen• money to someone you've never met.*

5. Pig butchering scams

This scam gets its name from the Chinese phrase 'Sha Zhu Pan', which means butchering a pig. Here, the victims are 'pigs' which are well-fed to fatten up before they are eventually butchered for their meat. In this scam, the victim is targeted through social media platforms like Instagram, Facebook, WhatsApp, or even professional networks like LinkedIn. The scammers first build a good rapport with the victims before persuading them to invest in a crypto platform controlled by them. Once they gain the trust of the 'pigs' and extract substantial investment from them, it is time to butcher the pig – i.e., cut off all contacts and vanish with the funds.

Sometimes, the episode does not end there. Scammers often try to siphon off even more money from the targets as fees to help recover the lost funds. According to Andrew Frey, a forensic financial analyst with the U.S. Secret Service - *It will become the costliest internet scam in the U.S. by dollars lost within a few short years if it hasn't done so already.*

6. Phishing scams

Most of us have 'won' the $10 million (or similar amounts) lottery and received an email confirmation, most likely from Nigeria. Many have lost a fortune while trying to receive the 'lottery' money. This is an old example of a phishing scam that has been used to cheat millions of people around the globe. This proven technique of deceiving people is used in crypto scams as well.

In a typical phishing scam, you are likely to receive an email or text message containing an external link (often resembling a genuine crypto website). Scammers often use logos, typefaces, and color schemes of genuine crypto platforms to make their websites and emails look authentic. Next, they would convince you to click on the link for a 'genuine purpose' like updating personal information without which your account may be deactivated. When you click on the link and input information, they can steal sensitive data like your login credentials for crypto platforms or even your private key. Before you realize it, the damage is done and cryptos are stolen from your wallet.

7. Upgrade scams

Crypto platforms like Ethereum can undergo multiple upgrades over the years. While upgrades make the platform more efficient and user-friendly, they present scammers with new opportunities. Scammers get in touch with unsuspecting investors to share their credentials on crypto exchanges to 'upgrade' their cryptos and then steal the cryptos. In some cases, scammers told victims to send a certain amount of cryptos so that their cryptos can be upgraded. Such scammers can pose as representatives of genuine crypto platforms like Ethereum or Bitcoin to gain your trust. Many Ethereum users fell victim to upgrade scams during the Merge.

8. Crypto giveaway scams

'Visit this Instagram page and pay a small processing fee to receive exciting free gifts' - sounds familiar? In crypto giveaway scams, scammers create fake crypto projects, websites, and social media pages to promote their projects. Next, targets are persuaded to follow certain prescribed steps to receive gifts like a large number of their tokens. The 'prescribed steps' generally involves paying a certain amount of cryptos as processing fee or even revealing sensitive information regarding your crypto wallets.

Many times, fraudsters hack the social media handles of large companies like Apple, as shown in Figure 23, to execute these giveaway scams. Also, look at the way they create urgency - 'only going on for the next 30 minutes'.

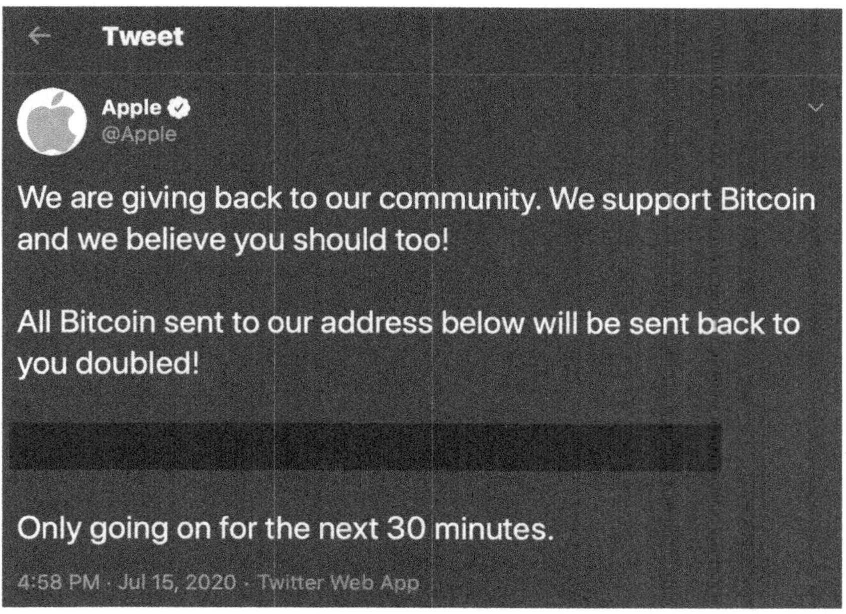

Figure 23: Crypto giveaway scam (Source: macrumors.com)

Crypto giveaways are generally announced on popular social media platforms like Facebook, Twitter, Instagram, and YouTube. They also misguide targets by using names, photos, and videos of important public figures (like actors, entrepreneurs, and TV personalities) to make their announcements look authentic. To lure genuine investors, bots and fake profiles join in the comment section to claim that they have received the giveaways.

9. Initial Coin Offering (ICO) scams

ICOs are the counterparts of Initial Public Offerings (IPOs) through which companies raise funds from the public. But in IPOs, the companies generally have a proven track record. In the case of ICOs, crypto platforms try to raise funds from the public even before they have any genuine operation. It's more like anyone can create a new coin that is then offered to the public to buy. The ICO boom in 2017/18 saw many fake crypto projects fooling investors by copying genuine crypto whitepapers, creating fake websites, and misguiding investors with fake celebrity endorsements.

Many of these scammers behind such ICOs often swiftly exit the market after raising funds. According to a study by Satis Group, an ICO advisory company, 80% of all ICOs launched in this period (2017/18) were fake. Developers behind such ICOs use stock images (a pre-existing image available for anyone to use) to show a fake team of advisors and executives. They also create a false sense of urgency to make you feel that you are going to miss out on an opportunity.

10. Fake exchanges and apps

Scammers not only create fake cryptos to dupe investors, they also often create fake crypto exchanges and mobile apps. The modus operandi is the same - they target investors through social media promotion, fake celebrity endorsements, and a combination of other means to direct investors toward the fake exchange or app. Once investors put their funds in the fake exchange to buy cryptos, scammers steal their money locking them out of the platforms.

These apps or exchanges generally promise a very high rate of return through their 'proprietary' trading technique. They can also impersonate real exchanges or apps. For example, in June 2022, Cybersecurity company CloudSEK unearthed a number of bogus crypto exchanges and apps that duped investors to the tune of $128 million. Some of these exchanges and apps impersonated the legitimate crypto exchange CoinEgg.

11. Crypto job scams

So you may be searching for a job and you have posted your resume on different job portals. Scammers get access to your contact details and contact you offering high paying 'jobs', some of which may be from the crypto industry. But guess what? To get the job you would be required to pay a certain amount of cryptos or fill out a detailed form revealing some personal information. Such information can be used to steal cryptos from your wallets. Crypto job scams have become very common these days.

12. AI-driven crypto scams

In April 2022, tech evangelist Elon Musk gave an interview with TED head Chris Anderson. During the conversation, the 50-year-old CEO of SpaceX and Tesla claimed that he launched a crypto project called BitVex. He also announced that anyone investing their cryptos in the project would receive a 30% return every day for the next 3 months. Anderson said he also had been receiving the promised 30% returns. Sounds great, right? After all, Musk, one of the staunchest supporters of cryptos and an entrepreneur par excellence, is behind the project. The only problem was, even Elon Musk himself had no idea he 'created' this super-profitable crypto platform. It was a DeepFake (an AI technique to create realistic videos or images) video made by scammers. They cloned Musk's voice and synced it with an original interview on a different subject altogether!

Figure 24: *A screengrab of Musk's DeepFake video (Source: bleepingcomputer.com)*

Artificial Intelligence (AI) tools have made it easier for scammers to cheat people through different means. AI-generated images, videos, and voice-overs can be very realistic and deceive people easily. Scammers are using AI to promote fake cryptos or exchanges and dupe investors.

Ethereum-Specific Scams

In addition to the general crypto scams, there are certain Ethereum-specific scams that investors, users, and developers need to be aware of.

Support scams

In this scam, someone from 'Ethereum Support' would contact you through a platform like Discord and try to resolve a technical problem. You are more likely to receive such messages when you post a query on a public Discord channel. Next, they would try to convince you that they belong to the genuine support team and would resolve your issues. Once they gain your trust, they would use tactics to make you reveal personal information like private keys or seed phrases (a random sequence of words that helps you recover your crypto wallet).

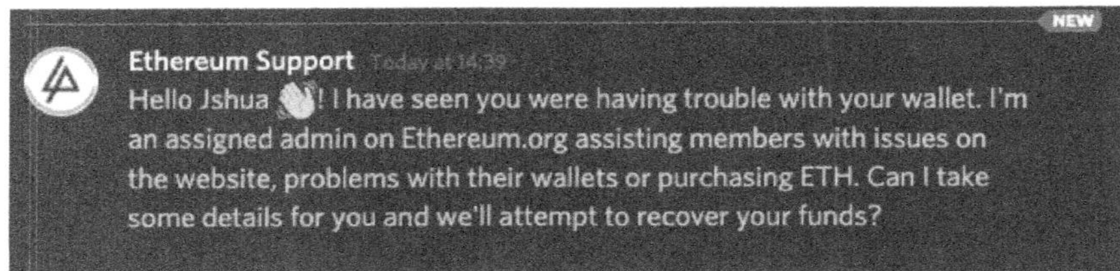

Figure 25: *Scammers impersonating the Ethereum support team (Source: Ethereum.org)*

ETH2 token scam

The Merge was a major Ethereum upgrade that was initially positioned as a transition to Ethereum 2.0 or ETH2. Unfortunately, many new investors were under the impression that their tokens need to be upgraded to ETH2. Leveraging this confusion, many scammers targeted investors asking them to deposit their ETH in certain addresses to get them upgraded to ETH2. However, there is no crypto called ETH2 and the Merge does not need any action by the investors owning ETH. Many investors lost money in this scam.

ETH mining pool scam

Even though Ethereum has migrated to Proof-of-Stake (PoS) which does not require mining, the mining pool scam continues to exist. In this scam, grifters would contact you to deposit your ETH in a mining pool which would be used to create more ETH and you would receive dividends. Of course, the promised dividends never come, and the scammers discontinue communication with the targets after receiving the cryptos.

Best practices to avoid crypto scams

Knowing about different common scams is half of the story, you need to follow certain best practices to be and stay in the safety zone.

Here are the main Do's and Don'ts of investing in cryptos

Do's

- ◇ Thoroughly research any new crypto project or token, via multiple genuine sources.
- ◇ Keep your cryptos in a cold wallet. It may be a little inconvenient to use but a cold wallet increases safety by manifold.
- ◇ Always use Two Factor Authentication (2FA) to prevent unauthorized access to your accounts.
- ◇ Always check the website URLs. A secure website starts with https rather than http. The additional 's' stands for a security certificate called Secure Sockets Layer (SSL).
- ◇ Stick to the most well-known cryptos and exchanges to avoid fraud.
- ◇ Before sending cryptos to anyone, make sure you are sending them to the right address. Once cryptos leave your wallet, there is nothing that you can do to reverse the transactions.
- ◇ Know the difference between ETH and ETC. When you are investing in 'Ethereum' you are talking about ETH. ETC or Ethereum Classic

is a separate token. The 2016 DAO hard fork discussed earlier in the book resulted in these two separate coins.

- Stick to Ethereum's official website (Ethereum.org) for announcements or to know about upgrades.
- It's always better to keep business separate from love and romance. If your online dating partner, whom you've never met, is suggesting you invest in a crypto project - it's time to be skeptical.
- Be suspicious of the 'Good Samaritan' 'living a lavish life on crypto earnings and offering to help you get rich faster.
- If you have fallen victim to a scam, immediately contact the law enforcement authorities through their official communication channels. In the USA, some of the agencies you can report to are the Federal Bureau of Investigation (FBI), Internet Crime Complaint Center (IC3), and the U.S. Securities and Exchange Commission (SEC).

Don'ts

- Never depend on a single source for information. Always verify it with multiple authoritative sources.
- Never invest in an unknown crypto project on an unknown exchange that is delivering 'astounding returns'.
- Never reveal your passwords, private keys, or seed phrase to anyone - not even to people claiming to be from the 'support team'.
- Don't believe in crypto projects delivering guaranteed high returns without any risk. When the expected return is higher, risk should be higher too. In the world of investing, 'guaranteed high return' is non-existent.
- Never download unknown apps or click on suspicious links received through emails or messages.

◇ No - Elon Musk or Cathie Wood is not giving away cryptos or promising astounding returns. Don't believe in celebrity endorsements or giveaways. They are most likely to be AI-generated or otherwise fake.

◇ Never pay to be hired for a job. Genuine companies -do not ask for payments before hiring you.

◇ Don't take unsolicited investing advice from strangers on social media. It's always better to acquire knowledge and do your own research before investing.

◇ Never invest in an ICO without doing due diligence - verifying the whitepaper, knowing about the key people behind the project, and analyzing their competitive advantage and the business model.

Now that you know how to keep your cryptos safe, it's time to create a strategy for your investments for maximum returns.

Let's now look at what an ideal crypto portfolio should look like.

Chapter 12

WHAT SHOULD AN IDEAL CRYPTO PORTFOLIO LOOK LIKE?

The essence of investment management is the management of risks, not the management of returns.
- *Benjamin Graham.*

The Babylonian Talmud, composed around 500 AD, is the primary source of Jewish religious laws. Over centuries, it has been the centerpiece of Jewish cultural life and served 'as the guide for the daily life' of Jews. Among commentaries on different aspects of life and philosophy, this ancient text of wisdom offers some investing lessons too. As one of the earliest notions of asset allocation, the Talmud says - *A man should always keep his wealth in three forms: one-third in real estate, another in merchandise, and the remainder in liquid assets.* It seems like portfolio management is not as modern as many of us would like to believe. More recently in 1738, Swiss mathematician and physicist Daniel Bernoulli observed - *it is advisable to divide goods that are exposed to some small danger into several small portions rather than to risk them all together.* This was a more classical version of the modern-day colloquial - *don't put all your eggs in one basket.* While at different times there have been different rules of thumb for allocating investible funds, the world was waiting for a more concrete approach.

In 1952, American economist Harry Max Markowitz, born to a Jewish family in 1929, published a paper titled 'Portfolio Selection' in The Journal of Finance. It applied a good dose of mathematics to analyze stock market returns. The paper later came to be known as the Modern Portfolio Theory (MPT). It demonstrated for the first time how an 'efficient' portfolio' can be developed to maximize return for a given level of risk. Over the last seven decades, MPT has been the cornerstone for developing portfolios and allocating assets. Today, it is the main instrument in every portfolio manager's toolbox. Markowitz, often cited as the father of modern finance, was awarded the prestigious Noble Prize in Economics in 1990 for this theory on portfolio allocation.

Historically, investing has been about finding some 'good bets' and then hoping that they multiply our investments. But there is no secret tool to find such sure-shot bets. Returns do not exist in isolation from risks. There is a risk-return trade-off, the relationship in which an investment offering a higher return invariably involves higher risks. Also, because of asymmetry, risks involved may even be higher than the potential rewards (more on this shortly). There are no perfect bets. The best option, as shown by Markowitz's celebrated theory, is to mix a variety of assets in a way that maximizes returns for a given risk level. So, how do we arrive at such asset combination?

The answer lies in the correlation of the assets.

Two assets are correlated when their returns move in tandem. For example, tech stocks like Microsoft and Alphabet are likely to have a high positive correlation. In fact, their 3-month correlation is 0.73 (as of April 2023). They operate under similar market conditions and their stock prices tend to respond to similar factors. However, two companies from different sectors like banking and pharma may have low correlation.

The idea of MPT is to diversify your funds into a set of assets that have a low positive, or even negative, correlation. So, when one asset does not perform well, another one compensates for it. This is how MPT prescribes diversification to spread risks across multiple assets.

Diversification is a catchword for any modern portfolio manager. It helps you manage your risk effectively while expecting the best possible return. In diversification, we don't look for sure-shot bets or look at assets in isolation. Rather, we try to build a portfolio of assets that maximizes returns while keeping associated risks low.

Cryptos as an alternative investment option

In investing, numbers speak louder than opinions. The benefits of diversification are well-established and empirically tested. A well-balanced portfolio can include not only different options from the same asset class but a number of different asset classes such as stocks, bonds, commodities, real estate, and gold. So, what about cryptos?

Profit-maximizing investors are in constant search of alternative investment options to supplement traditional assets. Over the last decade, cryptos have proved to be one of the most important alternative assets. But how do we evaluate the relevance of cryptos as a significant asset class? Here also, our guide is Markowitz's theory that has revolutionized portfolio management.

MPT has two central ideas - 1. diversification can lower overall risk. 2. we can develop an optimum portfolio by investing in assets that have low positive correlation. While cryptos provide an option for diversifying your portfolio, they also have a low correlation with traditional assets. According to Bloomberg's analysis, Bitcoin's 10-year correlation with Russell 3000 (which includes 3000 publiclytraded US stocks representing approximately 96% of the US stock market cap) is just 0.2. Its 10-year correlations with NASDAQ 100 or the Bloomberg Commodity Index are even lower - 0.18 and 0.06 respectively.

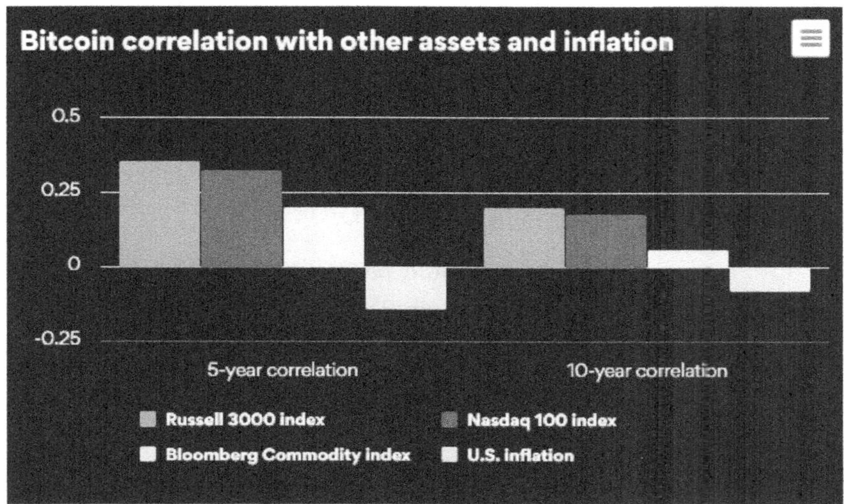

Figure 26: *Bitcoin's correlation with other assets (Source: Bloomberg)*

bitcoin, being the largest crypto by market cap and controlling about 45% of the crypto market, is a good proxy for the entire crypto market. So, according to MPT, cryptos can be an important alternative investment option. If we look at the overall performance of the crypto market, it has grown from a meager $14 billion in January 2017 (when cryptos really took off) to $1.26 trillion in April 2023. This is a whopping 9,000% growth in 6 years. Comparatively, the S&P 500 index grew by 78% in the same period from 2278.8 to 4055.9. If we look at the performance of gold, during this timeframe it provided a 74% return (from $1,150 to $2,000 per oz). So, despite the high volatility, a well-balanced crypto portfolio outperformed asset classes in this period.

Another reason to bet on cryptos as an alternative investment option is that cryptos provide a positive asymmetric bet. In a symmetrical bet, the size of your bet is equal to the reward. When you risk $100 for a potential gain of $100, it's a symmetrical bet. But when you bet $100 for a reward of $6 or $7, this is a negative asymmetry bet. Here, the potential reward is much lower than the money you are putting on the table.

However, if your $100 bet can potentially fetch you $5,000 or $10,000 - it can be a hugely positive asymmetric bet. So, a positive asymmetric bet is like a coin toss in which heads you win and tails you lose only a little. The upside potential of cryptos is so high that even if there is a possibility of cryptos going all the way down to 0, it still makes rational sense to put a small portion of your funds in cryptos.

So, how much of your funds should be in cryptos? And how do we allocate funds among different cryptos?

Let's find these answers.

Developing the right crypto portfolio

There is no one right answer to the question of how much of your funds should be in cryptos. It depends entirely on your financial goals, risk appetite, age, and income status. Depending on these factors, you can allocate 5-15% of your entire portfolio to crypto. The risk-takers or young investors may allocate on the higher side of this range, while people investing for retirement should be on the lower side. Remember that cryptos are high-risk investments and their volatility is much higher than stocks.

Now, for the next question - how to allocate funds among different cryptos. Here we can take a number of different approaches. But in all these approaches, we suggest allocating a lion's share to the top 2 players - bitcoin (BTC) and Ether (ETH).

50/50 portfolio

Firstly, a simple 50-50 crypto portfolio consisting of only BTC and ETH can work absolutely fine. BTC offers you a medium of exchange and a store of value. ETH offers these two in addition to a world of decentralized applications. Together, they pretty much cover everything cryptos have to offer. Currently (May 2023), the crypto market is valued at $1.26 trillion. Together BTC ($566 billion) and

ETH ($228 billion) control about 63% of this market cap.

60/40 portfolio

Let's consider the traditional 60/40 portfolio. It's generally used to allocate 60% of funds in stocks and 40% in fixed-income securities like bonds. However, the 60/40 rule can be applied in other situations in which we have 2 major options. If we keep our crypto exposure limited to only BTC and ETH, 60% in BTC and 40% in ETH or 60% in ETH and 40% in BTC can be another simplified crypto portfolio.

45/45/10 portfolio

If you don't want to miss out on some other coins, you can allocate 10% of your portfolio to these coins in addition to the top 2. In that case, your crypto portfolio will look like 45/45/10 in which 45% is invested in BTC, 45% in ETH, and the remaining 10% is experimented with other options. For this 10%, it's better to make your selection from the top 10 cryptos by market cap. Let the market decide the investment worthiness.

#	Coin	Price	1h	24h	7d	24h Volume	Mkt Cap
1	Bitcoin BTC	$28,965.41	0.3%	5.7%	-4.6%	$21,499,418,784	$560,54[illegible],476,410
2	Ethereum ETH	$1,915.55	0.4%	4.8%	-9.0%	$11,502,042,115	$230,57[illegible],130,455
3	Tether USDT	$1.00	0.1%	0.0%	0.1%	$28,843,119,691	$81,66[illegible],859,041
4	BNB BNB	$338.55	0.0%	2.4%	-1.3%	$819,777,000	$53,46[illegible],344,036
5	USD Coin USDC	$1.00	0.0%	0.0%	0.0%	$4,699,917,469	$30,68[illegible],462,964
6	XRP XRP	$0.473753	0.4%	3.7%	-10.8%	$1,226,292,209	$24,52[illegible],330,986
7	Cardano ADA	$0.406311	0.5%	7.0%	-8.4%	$314,532,640	$14,23[illegible],033,424
8	Lido Staked Ether STETH	$1,914.34	0.3%	5.0%	-9.2%	$24,104,944	$11,77[illegible],429,075
9	Dogecoin DOGE	$0.081791	0.3%	3.8%	-13.0%	$431,615,383	$11,37[illegible],344,608
10	Polygon MATIC	$1.03	1.0%	6.6%	-12.1%	$387,404,238	$9,51[illegible],656,892

Figure 27: *Top-10 cryptos by market cap (Source: coinmarketcap.com)*

What about a 100% ETH portfolio?

Zurich-based blockchain advisory company Verum Capital studied 7 different crypto portfolios to find out the best one. The study period was between the 2018 crypto bear market and the 2021 crypto bull market. Here are the interesting findings:

Portfolio 1: Splitting $1000 among the top 100 cryptos by market cap.

Result: Investment growth 22.6X.

Portfolio 2: Splitting $1000 among the top 100-200 cryptos by market cap.

Result: Investment growth 8.7X.

Portfolio 3: Splitting $1000 among the newly listed companies in the top 200.

Result: Investment growth 17.6X.

Portfolio 4: Splitting $1000 among the newly listed companies in Binance between 2018-Feb 2019.

Result: Investment growth 15.2X.

Portfolio 5: Investing $1000 entirely in BTC.

Result: Investment growth 18.7X.

Portfolio 6: Investing $1000 entirely in ETH.

Result: Investment growth 38.7X.

Portfolio 7: Splitting $1000 equally between ETH and BTC.

Result: Investment growth 28.7X.

Now, let's consider that in the same period, the total crypto market cap grew from $115 billion to $3 trillion, which is a 26X growth. We can see that Portfolio 6 (100% ETH) outperformed all combinations. Also, only Portfolio 6 (100% ETH) and Portfolio 7 (50/50 between ETH and BTC) outperformed the entire market.

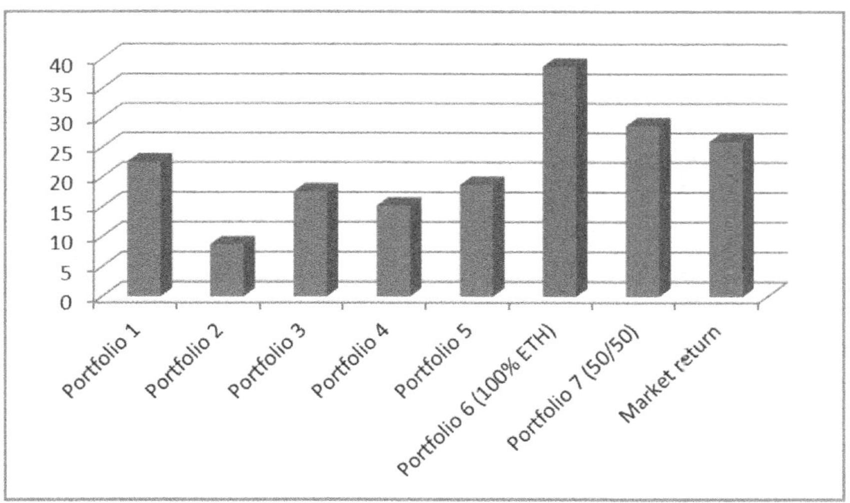

Figure 28: *Outperformance of the ETH-only portfolio (Data source: Verum Capital)*

So, the perfect portfolio for an ETH maximalist is allocating 100% of your crypto funds to ETH. BTC and ETH have a very high positive correlation. As of January 2023, the 3-month correlation between Bitcoin and Ethereum is 0.98, which is a near perfect positive correlation.

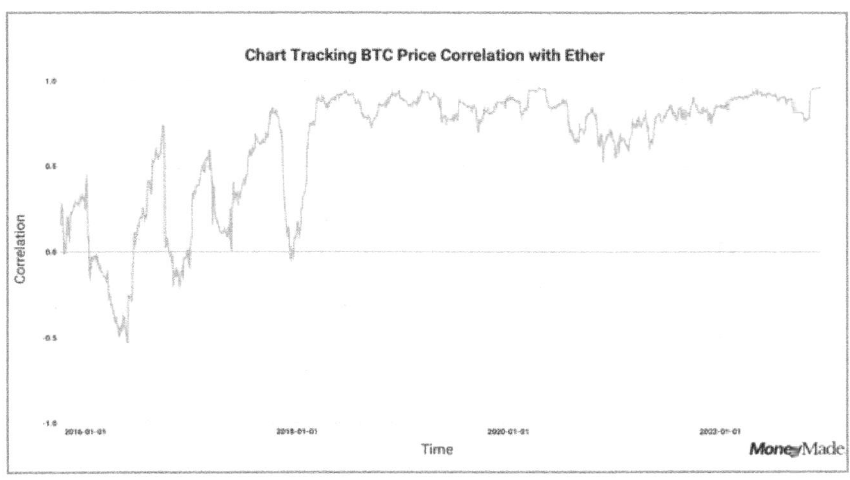

Figure 29: *BTC-ETH correlation (Source: MoneyMade)*

Therefore, going with a 100% Ethereum portfolio can also catch much of Bitcoin's gain, while you can bank on Ethereum's future potential as the de-facto market leader in a decentralized economy.

Now, let's look at another reason to be bullish about ETH. Guess what? it's least likely to be affected by tight crypto regulations.

Chapter 13

BUSTING MYTHS AROUND CRYPTO REGULATIONS

If crypto succeeds, it's not because it empowers better people. It's because it empowers better institutions.
- Vitalik Buterin.

It's not very common for Europe to become the first one to regulate a new industry. Most often, the US leads the way. But when it comes to regulating crypto, the former is heading the pack. In April 2023, the EU parliament passed the Markets in Crypto-Assets (MiCA) regulation. It addresses a broad range of concerns like consumer protection, money laundering, environmental effects, financial stability, and corporate reporting. Above all, the law wants to safeguard users against market manipulations and financial crimes. 517 lawmakers voted in favor while 38 voted against this Pan-EU crypto regulation. American multinational law firm Akin Gump calls MiCA 'one of the first attempts globally at comprehensive regulation of cryptocurrency markets'. MiCA's groundwork started in early 2018 at the height of a crypto boom. It was formally introduced 2 years later - in September 2020. Finally, the crypto industry in Europe gets a solid legal footing - setting a benchmark for the rest of the world to follow.

While the US is yet to have a comprehensive crypto law, the current government has been mulling over one for quite some time. In March 2022, US President Joe Biden put out an executive order to examine the risks and benefits of cryptocurrencies. The Biden administration has laid down six major areas to cover - consumer protection, financial stability, illicit activity, U.S. competitiveness, financial inclusion, and responsible innovation. A note from the law firm Paul, Weiss, Rifkind, Wharton & Garrison LLP says *we will see a••itional crypto-relate• sanctions gui•ance, enforcement actions, an• •esignations in the near term.*

In 2022, the then Chancellor of the Exchequer and current UK prime Minister Rishi Sunak expressed his ambition of making Britain a 'global hub for crypto asset technology'. In February 2023, the UK formally laid out a plan to regulate crypto industries. In this recent announcement, the government proposed a number of measures to bring crypto assets under the purview of traditional financial regulations. In April 2023, Andrew Griffith, economic secretary to the U.K. Treasury, revealed to CNBC that Britain is likely to introduce specific laws to regulate crypto in the next 12 months. In the words of the deputy governor of the Bank of England, Britain needs to *continue to bring these activities an• entities (cryptos) within regulation.* He added that new regulations would ensure *new stablecoins meet stan•ar•s equivalent to those expecte• of commercial bank money.*

Among other developed countries, Japan recently published a white paper on how to boost the country's crypto industry and protect consumers. Canada, too, has come up with stricter rules for crypto exchanges. In August 2022, the Canadian banking and insurance regulator Office of the Superintendent of Financial Institutions (OSFI) published the first federal rules for cryptos. In the developing world, Brazil enacted a new crypto law in December 2022. Under this law, many crypto assets (which are considered securities) will come under the purview of the Brazilian Securities and Exchange Commission (CVM). India, home to about 115 million crypto users, has introduced a crypto-specific tax in its 2022 Union Budget. The country has also recently put crypto transactions under its existing money laundering laws.

Countries around the globe are putting up more potent crypto laws.

Cryptos are no longer just a cyberpunk's technological plaything. It's a trillion-dollar asset class with millions of users, developers, and investors. In the world of finance, nothing like crypto has happened before - with an amalgamation of technology and finance. Thus, the existing laws and regulations are not adequate to regulate all aspects of cryptos.

For years, financial regulators have had different opinions regarding how to regulate this wild new thing. There have been debates regarding the nature of crypto assets - are they securities or commodities? Can the existing securities and investing laws successfully deal with cryptos? We have seen the first wave of regulations around the 2017/18 crypto booms and ICO craze. More recent catastrophic events like the implosion of TerraUSD (UST) and FTX have brought crypto regulations back on the table again. Naturally, we are likely to see more crypto-specific regulations, laws, and guidelines as this novel technology and a fast-growing alternative asset becomes more mainstream.

A lot of users and investors are concerned about crypto-related regulations. There is a common myth that regulations are universally bad for tan industry in which decentralization is a core element. We believe a comprehensive regulatory framework for all digital assets is actually good for the mass adoption of cryptos. Such regulations will help establish the trust of the majority in this technological innovation. This would help cryptos integrate with mainstream finance and investing. Moreover, there is a need for a mechanism to protect the interests of all stakeholders - investors, developers, and users. If we want to get rid of all sorts of frauds, scams, and other pitfalls, a healthy dose of regulations is the only way forward.

Lastly, an all-purpose blockchain like Ethereum is least likely to be affected by any such regulations.

Let's see why.

Regulations are not always bad

In his 40-year career as an American attorney and CEO, John J. Ray III has guided dozens of companies through bankruptcy proceedings. He was the one who handled Enron's liquidation process and handed over more than $20 billion of recovered funds to investors. Ray is also the court-appointed CEO of FTX to set its books in order after the epic downfall.

Shortly after being appointed, he didn't mince his words while talking about FTX- *Never in my career have I seen such a complete failure of corporate controls an• such a complete absence of trustworthy financial information as occurre• here. From compromise• systems integrity an• faulty regulatory oversight abroa• to the concentration of control in the han•s of a very small group of inexperience•, unsophisticate•, an• potentially compromise• in•ivi•uals, this situation is unprece•ente•.*

1 million investors from countries across the world lost more than $8 billion in the FTX saga. But strangely, investors from Japan still had some good news. They were the first set of FTX customers who were allowed to withdraw funds starting February 21, 2023. So, why was there an exception for Japanese investors? The answer lies in Japan's pragmatic set of crypto regulations. Among a bunch of other strict rules, crypto exchanges in Japan are required to keep customers' funds in a separate account from their own. Japan has been one of the front runners in regulating cryptos to protect the interest of investors.

The FTX episode proved Japan's approach to creating a regulatory balance is good for both the industry and its participants.

In 2022, cryptos underwent a tumultuous year driven by events shaking people's confidence. There was a brutal bear market. First, the implosion of TerraUSD (UST) and then the colossal failure of FTX dampened investors' sentiments further. Also, as we discussed in Chapter 11, crypto users have lost billions of dollars in scams, thefts, and fraud in recent years. Going forward it is very crucial to build trust and transparency in an asset category which is already considered high-risk. Today, when bank failures occur, institutions like the Federal Deposit Insurance Corporation (FDIC) step in to save US depositors(with limitations). However, when a crypto exchange collapses, investors have no such institutions to fall back on. The scams around ICOs in 2017/18 happened mostly because of lack of regulatory oversight. No industry can grow if the customers don't feel safe. Clearly laid out rules would create a level playing field, improve transparency and build investors' confidence.

Plus, a well-regulated industry would find it easier to integrate with the mainstream economy. A transparent industry would attract more users, developers, and investors. Moreover, when cryptos come under the supervision of dedicated regulators, more large-scale institutional investment is likely to flow into them. Regulations of cryptos can create a virtuous cycle in which comprehensive rules would enhance market adoption while large-scale adoption would lead to more crypto-friendly norms.

Lastly, the lack of a concrete regulatory framework can create uncertainty, which does no good to any business. Businesses need clarity. Recently, Coinbase CEO Brian Armstrong said *while the US has the potential to be an important market in crypto, it is not providing regulatory clarity*. He also added - *I think if a number of years go by where we don't see regulatory clarity around us ... we may have to consider investing more elsewhere in the world. Anything including, you know, relocating,.*

According to a Bloomberg report, Coinbase started talking to institutional clients in March 2023 to set up a crypto exchange overseas. In April, it obtained a license from the Bermuda Monetary Authority (BMA), which allows it to operate as a crypto exchange under its jurisdiction. Moreover, Coinbase has taken up a 'Go Broad, Go Deep' strategy under which it's actively seeking to augment operations outside the US. The world's second-largest crypto exchange has doubled down on its investments in Canada in recent months. And, Coinbase is not the only one exchange thinking of moving out of the US. Switzerland's Sygnum, the world's first digital bank, and Liechtenstein's Bank Frick have recently received a large number of requests, many of which are from the US, to open accounts in offshore companies.

Businesses need regulatory clarity to manage risks.

If we look at the current state of crypto regulations in major markets like the US, EU, and UK, the main driving forces behind them are consumer protection, financial stability, environmental protection, and transparency. In addition, such regulations are aiming to clamp down on illegal activities like money laundering. According to Andrew Griffith, Economic Secretary to the Treasury, *we remain stea•fast in our commitment to grow the economy an• enable technological change an• innovation – an• this inclu•es crypto asset technology. But we must also protect consumers who are embracing this new technology - ensuring robust, transparent, an• fair stan•ar•s.* Going by a note by the Biden administration, ... *new technologies nee• commensurate safeguar•s. Safeguar•s will ensure that new technologies are secure an• beneficial to all—an• that the new •igital economy works for the many, not just the few.* EU's newly passed crypto law MiCA says - *By enhancing the protection of consumers an• investors as well as financial stability, the regulation promotes innovation an• use of crypto-assets.* Changpeng Zhao, CEO of the world's largest crypto exchange Binance, said - MiCA is a *pragmatic solution to the challenges we collectively face.*

Pragmatic regulations can be a win-win for everyone involved in cryptos.

Ethereum is flexible enough to navigate tight regulations

In December 2022, 3 US lawmakers introduced the Crypto-Asset Environmental Transparency Act. Once enacted, this new law will direct the Environmental Protection Agency (EPA) to report on the energy usage and environmental impact of crypto miners. Such legislation aimed at curbing energy-intensive crypto mining is going to affect blockchains like Bitcoin, which run on Proof-of-Work (PoW). By switching to Proof of Stake (PoS), environmental regulations will not put a dent in Ethereum's operations. According to Scott Faber, The Environmental Working Group's (EWG) senior vice president for government affairs, *recently completed Ethereum Merge and past code changes show that....every industry, including the financial sector, can reduce its electricity use and greenhouse gas emissions.*

Ethereum has created a benchmark in terms of achieving energy efficiency.

Another major advantage Ethereum has over most other crypto platforms is that it's a general-purpose blockchain. Being a crypto marketplace also means Ethereum has more flexibility with respect to surviving in a tight regulatory environment. Ethereum does not have a specific set of applications and use cases. If tomorrow, in a highly unlikely case, there are regulations curbing the role of cryptos as a means of payment, it could be a death sentence for Bitcoin but not for Ethereum. Since any web-based application can be built on Ethereum, regulations on any specific area would not put it into an existential crisis. Ethereum has a plethora of non-financial applications too - like gaming and social networking. They are much less likely to be affected by even the strictest of financial regulations. To summarize - there can be restrictions on some specific applications (like cross-border large payments) but even an all-encompassing set of regulations shutting down an entire marketplace is highly unlikely.

We therefore believe that when consumers' interests are protected with a robust set of laws, it's going to be a bullish factor for cryptos in general. A safer and more predictable environment would not only attract more serious investors and businesses but also facilitate mainstreaming of this most promising financial innovation. In such a case, cryptos would create much greater value - a lion's share of which would emerge from the top-2 players in the market.

CONCLUSION: STAYING SANE AMONG THE CHAOS

The only certainty in crypto is uncertainty. So I'd like to end with some advice on maintaining your sanity during the future bull and bear markets to come.

First, don't allow yourself to be consumed with Ethereum, or crypto as a whole. I've talked to thousands of investors over the past decade and the happiest ones are always people whose investments are a part of who they are... not 100% of who they are. On the flipside those who embrace crypto as their entire personality hit the highest highs but also suffer from the lowest lows... both financially, mentally and spiritually.

Ethereum, like any other financial investment, is a one that will transfer wealth from the impatient to the patient. Checking price charts daily might give you that momentary dopamine hit you're looking for, but ultimately won't help you move closer to your goals. When in doubt, zoom out.

I can make one guarantee as well, we will see another crypto bear market in the next decade, and if you own Ethereum or plan on owning it – you must be prepared for volatility.

Since 2015, here are some of the volatility events Ethereum has undergone:

- ◇ 12 drawdowns of over 30%
- ◇ 5 drawdowns of over 50%
- ◇ 2 drawdowns of over 70%
- ◇ 1 drawdown of over 90%

The most important thing to take from this though, is that even with all these pullbacks, Ethereum and the entire cryptocurrency space continues to move into new highs. In 2021 alone we saw the value of the cryptocurrency industry go from $800 Billion to over $2.8 Trillion in just 10 months. Even today at $1.2 Trillion, the crypto market is worth the same as it was in early 2021.

For the bigger picture, I hope this book has not only cleared up misconceptions about Ethereum and the wider crypto ecosystem as a whole, but taught you some new ideas as well.

However if there is something you don't understand, you can email us at admin@freemanpublications.com if you would like something clarified. We answer every single reader's email.

The past 12 months were chaotic for crypto investors, so as we move into the next year (and hopefully the next bull market) we wish you the best of luck with your investing!

One final word from us. If this book has helped you in any way, we'd appreciate it if you left a review on Amazon.

Reviews are the lifeblood of our business. We read every single one and incorporate your feedback into our future book projects.

To leave an Amazon review, go to https://freemanpublications.com/leaveareview

ACKNOWLEDGEMENTS

This book is a team effort, and while I get to be the face of the business and receive all the kind messages from readers, I can't ignore the people who helped make this book what it was.

Thank you first to our content team for their writing, editing, and proofreading efforts and dealing with my persistent questions about specific changes needing to be made.

Thank you to Mark Greenberg, our superstar narrator, who has really become "the voice" of Freeman Publications over the past 3 years.

Thank you to the 520+ Freeman readers who participated in our advanced reader program for this book. Your notes and feedback were invaluable in going from the final draft to the finished product. A special shout out to the readers of Superhuman AI and Ben's Bites – 2 excellent newsletters

A special mention must go to two people. First, Vinay Narayanan for his help on the book content despite travelling to multiple continents, and working all hours of the day. Not only for this book, but to the entire Freeman community as a whole.

Then Carlota Wilhite for her incredibly detailed feedback, ranging from areas we didn't clarify well enough to pointing out that one of my original chapter titles was immature! Without your input, this book simply would not have been as good as it is today.

An additional thank you to our thousands of readers on social media for your words of encouragement throughout this project.

Finally, thank you to my family, whose initial uncertainty of "are you still doing that book thing" has blossomed into full support for my vision here at Freeman Publications. This means more than you will ever know.

Oliver

London, England
April 2023

REFERENCES

Chapter 01

- Editors, M. I. T. T. R. (2020, April 2). *Explainer: What is a blockchain?* MIT Technology Review. Retrieved May 3, 2023, from https://www.technologyreview.com/2018/04/23/143477/explainer-what-is-a-blockchain/
- Sergeenkov, A. (2023, February 14). *How •oes ethereum work?* CoinDesk Latest Headlines RSS. Retrieved May 3, 2023, from https://www.coindesk.com/learn/how-does-ethereum-work/
- Browne, R. (2021, May 10). *Ethereum: What is it an• how is it •ifferent from bitcoin?* CNBC. Retrieved May 3, 2023, from https://www.cnbc.com/2021/05/10/ethereum-what-is-it-and-how-is-it-different-to-bitcoin.html
- Mills, R. (2023, March 15). *Cryptocurrency's energy consumption problem.* RMI. Retrieved May 3, 2023, from https://rmi.org/cryptocurrencys-energy-consumption-problem/#:~:text=Bitcoin%20alone%20is%20estimated%20to,fuel%20used%20by%20US%20railroads.
- *Ethereum Energy Consumption.* ethereum.org. (n.d.). Retrieved May 3, 2023, from https://ethereum.org/en/energy-consumption/
- GeeksforGeeks. (2022, July 22). *What is Ethereum Virtual Machine an• how it works?* GeeksforGeeks. Retrieved May 3, 2023, from https://www.geeksforgeeks.org/what-is-ethereum-virtual-machine-and-how-it-works/

- *Global Decentralized Finance (DEFI) market size revenue to hit nearly* ... (n.d.). Retrieved May 3, 2023, from https://www.einnews.com/pr_news/612823280/global-decentralized-finance-defi-market-size-revenue-to-hit-nearly-232-20-billion-by-2030-zion-market-research

Chapter 02

- *Why Ethereum is poised for growth: A look at network activity.* ConsenSys. (2022, September 7). Retrieved May 4, 2023, from https://consensys.net/blog/metamask/metamask-institutional/why-ethereum-is-poised-for-growth-a-look-at-network-activity/
- Kauflin, J. (2018, July 25). *Why major cryptocurrency investors are betting heavily against Ethereum.* Forbes. Retrieved May 4, 2023, from https://www.forbes.com/sites/jeffkauflin/2018/07/25/why-major-cryptocurrency-investors-are-betting-heavily-against-ethereum/?sh=36c378985d83
- Popper, N. (2017, February 27). *Business Giants to announce creation of a computing system based on Ethereum.* The New York Times. Retrieved May 4, 2023, from https://www.nytimes.com/2017/02/27/business/dealbook/ethereum-alliance-business-banking-security.html
- *The DAO: What was the DAO hack?* Gemini. (n.d.). Retrieved May 4, 2023, from https://www.gemini.com/cryptopedia/the-dao-hack-makerdao#section-what-is-a-dao
- *A brief history of ethereum.* Coin Rivet. (2021, July 30). Retrieved May 4, 2023, from https://coinrivet.com/guides/altcoins/a-brief-history-of-ethereum/
- Evans, J. (2015, August 1). *Vapor no more: Ethereum has launched.* TechCrunch. Retrieved May 4, 2023, from *https://techcrunch.com/2015/08/01/vapor-no-more-ethereum-has-launched/*

◇ Finley, K. (2014, January 27). Out in The open: Teenage hacker transforms web into one giant bitcoin network. Wired. Retrieved May 4, 2023, from https://www.wired.com/2014/01/ethereum/

Chapter 03

◇ Miller, C. (2021, October 28). *Stuart Haber an• Scott Stornetta: How our timestamping mechanism was use• in bitcoin.* CoinGeek. Retrieved May 4, 2023, from https://coingeek.com/stuart-haber-and-scott-stornetta-how-our-timestamping-mechanism-was-used-in-bitcoin-video/

◇ Reiff,N.(2022,July13).*Howmuchofallmoneyisinbitcoin?*Investopedia. Retrieved May 4, 2023, from https://www.investopedia.com/tech/how-much-worlds-money-bitcoin/#:~:text=A%20bitcoin%20was%20worth%20%2454%2C572,2.9%25%20of%20the%20world's%20money.

◇ Ossinger, J. (2022, January 6). *Ethereum's •ominance in •efi is 'far from given,' JPMorgan says.* Bloomberg.com. Retrieved May 4, 2023, from https://www.bloomberg.com/news/articles/2022-01-06/ethereum-s-dominance-in-defi-is-far-from-given-jpmorgan-says

◇ *Creighton University - The Economist.* (n.d.). Retrieved May 4, 2023, from https://www.economist.com/sites/default/files/creighton_university_kraken_case_study.pdf

◇ Burke, E. (2021, May 13). *Microsoft calls time on Azure blockchain-as-a-service.* Silicon Republic. Retrieved May 4, 2023, from https://www.siliconrepublic.com/enterprise/microsoft-azure-blockchain-as-a-service-consensys-quorum-ethereum

◇ ForbesIndia. (n.d.). *Global bitcoin payments market to increase by 16.3% annually between 2022 an• 2031.* Forbes India. Retrieved May 4, 2023, from https://www.forbesindia.com/article/cryptocurrency/global-bitcoin-payments-market-to-increase-by-163-annually-between-2022-and-2031/80807/1

- Abrol, A. (2023, March 10). *How many bitcoins are there and how many are left to mine?* Blockchain Council. Retrieved May 4, 2023, from https://www.blockchain-council.org/cryptocurrency/how-many-bitcoins-are-left/#:~:text=There%20is%20a%20limited%20supply,million%20left%20to%20be%20mined.
- Yahoo! (n.d.). *Valid points: Why ether doesn't need a supply cap to hedge against inflation.* Yahoo! Finance. Retrieved May 4, 2023, from https://finance.yahoo.com/news/valid-points-why-ether-doesn-123000309.html#:~:text=Like%20bitcoin%2C%20ether%20has%20a,is%20programmed%20to%20increase%20gradually.
- Rene Millman, S. G. (2022, June 4). *What is Ethereum 2.0? Ethereum's consensus layer and merge explained*. Decrypt. Retrieved May 4, 2023, from https://decrypt.co/resources/what-is-ethereum-2-0
- GeeksforGeeks. (2022, December 22). *Consensus algorithms in Blockchain.* GeeksforGeeks. Retrieved May 4, 2023, from https://www.geeksforgeeks.org/consensus-algorithms-in-blockchain/

Chapter 04

- Hagiu, A., & Wright, J. (2021, November 4). Will network effects Save Ethereum from the Ethereum Killers? Will network effects save Ethereum from the Ethereum killers? Retrieved May 4, 2023, from https://platformchronicles.substack.com/p/will-network-effects-save-ethereum
- Skur, A. (2023, January 25). Ethereum (ETH) blockchain developer numbers record 5x increase. DailyCoin. Retrieved May 4, 2023, from https://dailycoin.com/ethereum-eth-blockchain-developer-numbers-record-5x-increase/
- *The half-truth of first-mover advantage.* Harvard Business Review. (2014, August 1). Retrieved May 4, 2023, from https://hbr.org/2005/04/the-half-truth-of-first-mover-advantage

- *Ethereum will soon have 100 million a••resses with non-zero balance – what this milestone means for eth price.* Crypto News. (n.d.). Retrieved May 4, 2023, from https://cryptonews.com/news/ethereum-will-soon-have-100-million-addresses-with-non-zero-balance-what-this-milestone-means-for-eth-price.htm#:~:text=Over%20the%20last%20three%20years,will%20undoubtedly%20be%20big%20news.
- Asmakov, A. (2023, January 17). *Ethereum smart contracts •eployment jumpe• 293% in 2022: Alchemy Developer Report.* Decrypt. Retrieved May 4, 2023, from https://decrypt.co/119371/ethereum-smart-contracts-deployment-jumped-293-2022-alchemy-developer-report
- Best, R. de. (2023, April 24). *DEFI TVL history 2018-2023.* Statista. Retrieved May 4, 2023, from https://www.statista.com/statistics/1272181/defi-tvl-in-multiple-blockchains/
- *Economic moat.* Wall Street Prep. (2022, November 21). Retrieved May 4, 2023, from https://www.wallstreetprep.com/knowledge/economic-moat/
- Srivastav, A. K. (2023, January 19). *Economic moat.* WallStreetMojo. Retrieved May 4, 2023, from https://www.wallstreetmojo.com/economic-moat/

Chapter 05

- Team, S. C. (2023, February 28). *What is Ethereum's Shanghai upgra•e?: Shar•eum.* Shardeum Blogs | EVM-based Sharded L1 Blockchain. Retrieved May 4, 2023, from https://shardeum.org/blog/ethereum-shanghai-upgrade/
- Phillips, G. (2022, September 15). *The Ethereum merge is complete-but will it make ethereum gas fees cheaper?* MUO. Retrieved May 4, 2023, from https://www.makeuseof.com/ethereum-merge-complete/

- Canny, W. (2022, October 13). *Ether becomes deflationary for first time since the merge: Coinbase.* CoinDesk Latest Headlines RSS. Retrieved May 4, 2023, from https://www.coindesk.com/markets/2022/10/13/ether-becomes-deflationary-for-first-time-since-the-merge-coinbase/
- Redman, J. (2023, February 3). *Ethereum network's rising gas fees in 2023: A balancing act of growth and cost.* Bitcoin News. Retrieved May 4, 2023, from https://news.bitcoin.com/ethereum-networks-rising-gas-fees-in-2023-a-balancing-act-of-growth-and-cost/
- Cointelegraph. (2023, February 8). *Ethereum gas price spikes 29% in January as user activity grows: Report by Cointelegraph.* Investing.com. Retrieved May 4, 2023, from https://www.investing.com/news/cryptocurrency-news/ethereum-gas-price-spikes-29-in-january-as-user-activity-grows-report-2998245
- *Layer 2.* ethereum.org. (n.d.). Retrieved May 4, 2023, from https://ethereum.org/en/layer-2/
- *Ethereum Sharding explained.* district0x Education Portal. (2018, October 24). Retrieved May 4, 2023, from https://education.district0x.io/general-topics/understanding-ethereum/ethereum-sharding-explained/
- *The Beacon Chain.* ethereum.org. (n.d.). Retrieved May 4, 2023, from https://ethereum.org/en/roadmap/beacon-chain/
- *Ethereum Roadmap.* ethereum.org. (n.d.). Retrieved May 4, 2023, from https://ethereum.org/en/roadmap/#:~:text=What%20are%20Ethereum%20upgrades%3F,from%20across%20the%20Ethereum%20ecosystem.

Chapter 06

- Chittum, M. (2023, January 18). *'Dr Doom' Nouriel Roubini says 'literally 90% of crypto is a scam' and Sam Bankman-fried and FTX are not outliers in the market.* Business Insider. Retrieved May 4, 2023, from https://www.businessinsider.in/investment/news/

dr-doom-nouriel-roubini-says-literally-90-of-crypto-is-a-scam-and-sam-bankman-fried-and-ftx-are-not-outliers-in-the-market/articleshow/97100543.cms

- Robertson, H. (n.d.). *JPMorgan Backs Bitcoin to rise 28% an• says cryptocurrencies are now its preferre• alternative asset.* Business Insider. Retrieved May 4, 2023, from https://markets.businessinsider.com/news/currencies/bitcoin-outlook-jpmorgan-cryptocurrencies-alternative-assets-2022-5
- *Global cryptocurrency ownership •ata 2023 - Triplea.* Triple. (2023, April 14). Retrieved May 4, 2023, from https://triple-a.io/crypto-ownership-data/
- Smith, T. (2023, January 5). *FTX: An overview of the exchange an• its collapse.* Investopedia. Retrieved May 4, 2023, from https://www.investopedia.com/ftx-exchange-5200842
- *How many cryptocurrency exchanges are there?* Cryptimi. (2021, July 27). Retrieved May 4, 2023, from https://www.cryptimi.com/guides/how-many-cryptocurrency-exchanges-are-there
- Blackstone, T. (2022, November 3). *How to protect your crypto in 2023.* Security.org. Retrieved May 4, 2023, from https://www.security.org/crypto/protection/
- Quarmby, B. (2022, August 3). *Solana-base• wallet hack saw millions •raine•.* Cointelegraph. Retrieved May 4, 2023, from https://cointelegraph.com/news/ongoing-solana-based-wallet-hack-has-already-seen-millions-drained

Chapter 07

- Valente, M. (2022, October 5). *Ethereum Price: Real-time price changes in ETH.* Coinhouse. Retrieved May 4, 2023, from https://www.coinhouse.com/ethereum-price/

- Somraaj, S. (2022, September 22). Ethereum token issuance plummets 95% following merge. Decrypt. Retrieved May 4, 2023, from https://decrypt.co/110331/ethereum-token-issuance-plummets-95-following-merge
- Black, S. (n.d.). *The time Mark Twain went broke provides some interesting investing lessons.* Business Insider. Retrieved May 4, 2023, from https://www.businessinsider.com/the-time-mark-twain-went-broke-provides-some-interesting-investing-lessons-2018-1?IR=T
- *Ethereum (ETH) correlation with bitcoin at its monthly high, here's why this is good trend*. U.Today. (2023, March 30). Retrieved May 4, 2023, from https://u.today/ethereum-eth-correlation-with-bitcoin-at-its-monthly-high-heres-why-this-is-good-trend#:~:text=According%20to%20data%20from%20IntoTheBlock,Q1%20on%20a%20positive%20note.
- *How the merge impacted ETH Supply*. ethereum.org. (n.d.). Retrieved May 4, 2023, from https://ethereum.org/en/roadmap/merge/issuance/
- Nambiampurath, R. (2023, March 14). *Ethereum deflation accelerates to new record six months post merge.* BeInCrypto. Retrieved May 4, 2023, from https://beincrypto.com/ethereum-deflation-accelerates-new-record-six-months-post-merge/
- Jha, P. (2023, February 15). *Ethereum supply plunges 37% on crypto exchanges post the merge upgrade.* Cointelegraph. Retrieved May 4, 2023, from https://cointelegraph.com/news/ethereum-supply-plunges-37-on-crypto-exchange-post-the-merge-upgrade

Chapter 08

- Decentralized Finance Market Size, Scope, Growth and Profit-Sources Report to 2031. (n.d.). Retrieved May 4, 2023, from https://www.insightaceanalytic.com/report/decentralized-finance-market/1607

◇ Hicks, C. (n.d.). *Yiel• farming: An investing strategy involving staking or len•ing crypto assets to generate returns.* Business Insider. Retrieved May 4, 2023, from https://www.businessinsider.com/personal-finance/yield-farming?IR=T

◇ Roberts, J. J. (2023, April 13). *Intro•ucing fortune's crypto 40: Blockchain businesses built to last.* Fortune Crypto. Retrieved May 4, 2023, from https://fortune.com/crypto/2023/04/10/fortune-crypto-40-blockchain-companies-nonprofits-decentralized-collectives/

◇ Shivsak. (2023, March 27). *Real-worl• crypto: How •efi can help Millions of farmers in Africa an• In•ia.* Medium. Retrieved May 4, 2023, from https://entrepreneurshandbook.co/real-world-crypto-how-defi-can-help-millions-of-farmers-in-africa-and-india-6088a8cd3ec

◇ Coinbase. (n.d.). *What is Uniswap?* Coinbase. Retrieved May 4, 2023, from https://www.coinbase.com/learn/crypto-basics/what-is-uniswap

◇ *How ETHERISC is insuring Kenyans Farms.* Techpoint Africa. (2022, April 27). Retrieved May 4, 2023, from https://techpoint.africa/2022/04/21/decentralised-insurance-kenya-etherisc/

◇ DeSilver, D. (2023, May 2). *Most U.S. bank failures have come in a few big waves.* Pew Research Center. Retrieved May 4, 2023, from https://www.pewresearch.org/fact-tank/2023/04/11/most-u-s-bank-failures-have-come-in-a-few-big-waves/#:~:text=Outside%20of%20those%20two%20crisis,3.6%20between%202015%20and%202022.

◇ *Defi insurance: The next generation of insurance.* Hedera. (n.d.). Retrieved May 4, 2023, from https://hedera.com/learning/decentralized-finance/defi-insurance

◇ *Guest post by Footprint Analytics: 25 stats about the Defi In•ustry in 2022.* Crockett, Z. (2021, March 7). Why nfts are suddenly selling for millions of dollars. The Hustle. Retrieved May 4, 2023, from https://thehustle.co/why-nfts-are-suddenly-selling-for-millions-of-dollars/CoinMarketCap. (n.d.). Retrieved May 4, 2023, from https://coinmarketcap.com/community/

articles/63bf7d6aaa3e6b675443956a/

Chapter 09

- Lee, I. (n.d.). *Luxury NFTS coul• become a $56 billion market by 2030 an• coul• see '•ramatically' increase• •eman• thanks to the Metaverse, Morgan Stanley says.* Business Insider. Retrieved May 4, 2023, from https://markets.businessinsider.com/news/currencies/luxury-nfts-metaverse-56-billion-market-revenue-2030-morgan-stanley-2021-11
- *5 critical challenges nfts still nee• to overcome.* World Economic Forum. (n.d.). Retrieved May 4, 2023, from https://www.weforum.org/agenda/2021/08/nft-boom-cryptocurrency-digital-collectible-artwork?DAG=3&gclid=CjwKCAjw8-OhBhB5EiwADyoY1c9kePPnCGYUsquHUnBaWpWAPTSRuweLVGRpFU3qiSJzuK02IdCTXRoCQ94QAvD_BwE
- Crockett, Z. (2021, March 7). *Why nfts are su••enly selling for millions of •ollars.* The Hustle. Retrieved May 4, 2023, from https://thehustle.co/why-nfts-are-suddenly-selling-for-millions-of-dollars/
- Reyburn, S. (2019, May 16). Jeff Koons 'rabbit' sets auction record for most expensive work by living artist. The New York Times. Retrieved May 4, 2023, from https://www.nytimes.com/2019/05/15/arts/jeff-koons-rabbit-auction.html
- Geylan, Z. (2023, January 26). *Research: NFTS accounte• for 28% of the ETH gas usage in January.* CryptoSlate. Retrieved May 4, 2023, from https://cryptoslate.com/research-nfts-accounted-for-28-of-the-eth-gas-usage-in-january/
- Hunt, S. (2022, August 1). *Pearson Boss eyes nft texbooks as next revenue stream.* Evening Standard. Retrieved May 4, 2023, from https://www.standard.co.uk/business/pearson-andy-bird-nft-texbooks-business-opportunity-b1015938.html

◇ Dwarika, K. (2023, January 31). *What are nfts (non-fungible tokens)?* Rumie. Retrieved May 4, 2023, from https://learn.rumie.org/jR/bytes/what-are-nf-ts-non-fungible-tokens?gclid=CjwKCAjw0N6hBhAUEiwAXab-Te92E1lvjjboKeHw3nlljEvIHxWNrMzugxE5kGwegb-PMZOZOgQfGhoCdjYQAvD_BwE

◇ Lee, I. (n.d.). *Luxury NFTS coul• become a $56 billion market by 2030 an• coul• see '•ramatically' increase• •eman• thanks to the Metaverse, Morgan Stanley says.* Business Insider. Retrieved May 4, 2023, from https://markets.businessinsider.com/news/currencies/luxury-nfts-metaverse-56-billion-market-revenue-2030-morgan-stanley-2021-11

◇ Crockett, Z. (2021, March 7). *Why nfts are su••enly selling for millions of •ollars.* The Hustle. Retrieved May 4, 2023, from https://thehustle.co/why-nfts-are-suddenly-selling-for-millions-of-dollars/

Chapter 10

◇ Breitman, K. (2023, April 6). Ethereum, arbitrum, and why L2 solutions are a mess. Fortune Crypto. Retrieved May 4, 2023, from https://fortune.com/crypto/2023/04/05/ethereum-arbitrum-and-why-l2-solutions-are-such-a-mess/

◇ *Layer 2.* ethereum.org. (n.d.). Retrieved May 4, 2023, from https://ethereum.org/en/layer-2/

◇ Haig, B. S. (2023, March 17). *Daily layer 2 transaction count soars to recor• 1.54m.* The Defiant. Retrieved May 4, 2023, from https://thedefiant.io/ethereum-l2-txs-surpass-mainnet

◇ Adler, J. (2019, May 14). *The state of Ethereum Layer-2 protocol •evelopment #1.* Medium. Retrieved May 4, 2023, from https://media.consensys.net/the-state-of-ethereum-layer-2-protocol-development-2-f22b2603abd6?gi=f02da1751b15

◇ *Ethereum me•ian transaction fee chart.* BitInfoCharts. (n.d.). Retrieved May 4, 2023, from https://bitinfocharts.com/comparison/ethereum-median_transaction_fee.html#3y

◇ Monnot, B. (2022, February 24). Understanding rollup economics from first principles. Retrieved May 4, 2023, from https://barnabe.substack.com/p/understanding-rollup-economics-from?s=r

Chapter 11

◇ Hetler, A. (2023, April 19). 10 common cryptocurrency scams in 2023. WhatIs.com. Retrieved May 4, 2023, from https://www.techtarget.com/whatis/feature/Common-cryptocurrency-scams#:~:text=Ponzi%20schemes,-Ponzi%20schemes%20pay&text=To%20get%20fresh%20investors%2C%20cryptocurrency,huge%20profits%20with%20little%20risk.

◇ Johnson, H. (2023, March 29). *What are the most popular crypto scams to watch for in 2023| time stamped*. Time. Retrieved May 4, 2023, from https://time.com/personal-finance/article/popular-crypto-scams/

◇ Genç, E. (2022, December 10). *Crypto romance scams: Don't fall for these dating App Swindlers.* CoinDesk Latest Headlines RSS. Retrieved May 4, 2023, from https://www.coindesk.com/learn/crypto-romance-scams-dont-fall-for-these-dating-app-swindlers/

◇ Team, E. (2023, May 4). *E-Coin: Pump and dump scam coin or misunderstood gem?* Coin Bureau. Retrieved May 4, 2023, from https://www.coinbureau.com/analysis/e-coin-pump-dump-scam-coin-misunderstood-gem/

◇ *Scammers use Elon Musk deepfake to steal crypto.* VICE. (2022, May 27). Retrieved May 4, 2023, from https://www.vice.com/en/article/v7d5y9/scammers-use-elon-musk-deepfake-to-steal-crypto

Chapter 12

◇ Best crypto portfolio allocation tips for 2023. Techopedia. (2023, April 28). Retrieved May 4, 2023, from https://www.techopedia.com/cryptocurrency/best-crypto-portfolio-allocation

◇ Capital, V. (2023, March 15). *"what if I just invest in all the coins of the top 100 an• wait?""What if I just spot buy $eth an• hol•?""What if I only choose recent binance listings?"7 CMC •ata-•riven portfolio simulations + 6 key conclusions to prepare for next bull pic.twitter.com/arwz3e8pct.* Twitter. Retrieved May 4, 2023, from https://twitter.com/verumcapital/status/1635982856915697665

◇ Rhodes, J. (2021, September 3). *Bitcoin: The asymmetric bet (cryptocurrency: BTC-USD).* Seeking Alpha. Retrieved May 4, 2023, from https://seekingalpha.com/article/4453516-bitcoin-the-asymmetric-bet

◇ Tatar, J. (2021, December 18). *Cryptocurrencies as an alternative investment.* The Balance. Retrieved May 4, 2023, from https://www.thebalancemoney.com/cryptocurrencies-are-the-new-alternative-investment-4048017

◇ *Uncorrelate• assets explaine•: The low-risk, high-rewar• portfolio unicorns.* MoneyMade. (2023, February 14). Retrieved May 4, 2023, from https://moneymade.io/learn/article/uncorrelated-assets-explained

◇ *What is an asymmetric bet an• how can you use them to strive for better investment returns?* Endeavour Wealth Management. (n.d.). Retrieved May 4, 2023, from https://www.endeavourwealth.ca/post/what-is-an-asymmetric-bet-and-how-can-you-use-them-to-strive-for-better-investment-returns

◇ Duggan, W. (2023, April 15). *Nobel prize winners Markowitz an• Shiller •evelop the perfect portfolio through •iversification - Apple (NASDAQ:AAPL).* Benzinga. Retrieved May 4, 2023, from https://www.benzinga.com/general/education/14/11/4980296/nobel-prize-winners-perfect-portfolio-the-secret-ingredient-revealed-1

◇ Sponsored. (2021, October 30). *Mo•ern portfolio theory an• the efficient crypto portfolio.* Crypto Briefing. Retrieved May 4, 2023, from https://cryptobriefing.com/modern-portfolio-theory-and-the-efficient-crypto-portfolio/

- Manohar, A. (2023, April 27). *Gol• price regains $2000 level after ease in US •ollar. shoul• you buy?* mint. Retrieved May 4, 2023, from https://www.livemint.com/market/commodities/gold-price-regains-2000-level-after-ease-in-us-dollar-should-you-buy-11682565419992.html

Chapter 13

- ForbesIndia. (n.d.). *US lawmakers intro•uce a bill for EPA to investigate energy consumption by crypto mining.* Forbes India. Retrieved May 4, 2023, from https://www.forbesindia.com/article/cryptocurrency/us-lawmakers-introduce-a-bill-for-epa-to-investigate-energy-consumption-by-crypto-mining/81799/1
- Browne, R. (2023, April 20). *EU lawmakers approve worl•'s first comprehensive framework for Crypto Regulation.* CNBC. Retrieved May 4, 2023, from https://www.cnbc.com/2023/04/20/eu-lawmakers-approve-worlds-first-comprehensive-crypto-regulation.html
- The United States Government. (n.d.). *The a•ministration's roa•map to mitigate cryptocurrencies' risks.* The White House. Retrieved May 4, 2023, from https://www.whitehouse.gov/nec/briefing-room/2023/01/27/the-administrations-roadmap-to-mitigate-cryptocurrencies-risks/
- *A quick profile on John Ray III, the new CEO of FTX.* cnbctv18.com. (2022, November 19). Retrieved May 4, 2023, from https://www.cnbctv18.com/cryptocurrency/ftx-new-ceo-john-ray-iii-a-quick-profile-15203471.htm
- *FTX Japan lets customers with•raw fun•s, but many say they're still ...* (n.d.). Retrieved May 4, 2023, from https://www.thestreet.com/crypto/news/ftx-japan-lets-customers-withdraw-funds-but-many-say-theyre-still-locked-out

- Nakamichi, T., Sano, N., & Benny-Morrison, A. (2023, February 21). *FTX unit in Japan becomes first to resume customer with•rawals.* Bloomberg.com. Retrieved May 4, 2023, from https://www.bloomberg.com/news/articles/2023-02-21/ftx-unit-in-japan-becomes-first-to-resume-customer-withdrawals
- Linares, M. G. S. (2023, May 2). *Coinbase sets up shop in Bermu•a as it battles SEC at home.* Forbes. Retrieved May 4, 2023, from https://www.forbes.com/sites/digital-assets/2023/05/02/coinbase-sets-up-shop-in-bermuda-as-it-battles-sec-at-home/
- https://www.coindesk.com/business/2023/03/14/banking-crisis-in-us-likely-to-push-crypto-firms-offshore/

Made in United States
Orlando, FL
05 January 2024